The New Turnaround

THE NEW TURNAROUND

A Breakthrough for People, Profits and Change

Leonard Bertain, Ph.D.

North River Press
Croton-on-Hudson, New York

Additional copies of this book may be obtained
from your local bookstore or the publisher:
North River Press
Box 309
Croton-on-Hudson, NY 10520
Tel: (800)486-2665

For more information on the concepts and processes described in this book please
contact: **American Productivity Group**
561 Oakland Avenue
Oakland, CA 94610
Tel: (510) 653-6355

Copyright 1993 Leonard Bertain

No Blame is a registered trademark of American Productivity Group
No Excuses is a registered trademark of American Productivity Group

All rights reserved.
Except for the usual review purposes, no part of this work may be
reproduced or transmitted in any form or by any means, electronic or mechanical,
including photocopy, recording,
or any information retrieval system, without the permission
of the publisher.

Manufactured in the United States of America

ISBN: 0-88427-096-3

To my wife, Mary, who was
patient in bearing with me
while this book and my
consulting practice were evolving.
I love you.

Len

Introduction

Coming up with a title for this book was hard. I wanted to tell a story and use it as a way of illustrating a unique process for improving business. And I wanted this process to be understandable to a wide audience. But there weren't any familiar terms to explain it. Then I realized that the whole process described in this book addresses the issue of turning around a business. It may be a troubled business, as is the case described in the book, or it may be a business that wants to improve its operation.

Either case amounts to a turnaround in the way we manage a business, and the discovery that acting on good ideas of employees leads to a change in the way we look at the work of an organization. We are not talking about just any work; we are talking about "the right work." And when we do this, we find that the resultant organization is different, is turned around from its predecessor. The new organization focuses on understanding the value-adding functions of the business. This leads quickly to a highly productive structure with the ability to change in response to market demands, which in turn leads to greater profits.

In the traditional business sense, "turnaround," or the "turnaround expert," are terms that have negative connotations. The turnaround process in these terms is one in which the "expert" arrives at the door of the troubled company and begins the turnaround process by cutting costs and firing people. That is not what this turnaround is about. This turnaround process is systemic yet humanistic. To differentiate between the usage of turnaround in this title and its pejorative implications of the past we have dubbed it *The New Turnaround.*

This book addresses the issue of maximizing the most underutilized asset of a corporation—the people, by describing a new process of organizational change with an improved system of getting work done. Alternative measures of the organization are introduced that provide powerfully simple techniques, including Yes/No Charts and World Record Reports.

Interestingly, the process does not begin by asking the question "How can we make the work more efficient?" It starts with a more fundamental question: "What is the right work?"

These two questions lead the improvement process in diametrically opposite directions. We know where the first one leads us; Peters and Drucker talk about that. This book describes the alternate journey of change. It does so from the perspective of a worker who is involved in the process. As the story unfolds, the changing organization has a different look; it is a very good place to work, and it is more profitable.

The reader who has never experienced *The New Turnaround* may dismiss the story line as a number of unreal situations. However, you will be surprised at how real the story line is when you begin your own turnaround. Believe; this book is very real. It is the consolidation of a number of experiences I have had in real life with real people. I have used this process effectively in a wide variety of many businesses, from manufacturers, machine shops and distribution companies to government agencies, hospitals and banks. Most of the events are real. I have changed the names and some specific events in the story to assure anonymity.

As you find out quickly in the book, the process described is a form of discovery for the participants. Each step is a new discovery. It is an enjoyable but difficult journey. The uncertainty of the next step of discovery is painful for those who wish to preserve their old habits and systems. But the new system is more efficient, more productive and more comfortable for employees, as everyone is focused on maximizing the value delivered by the business. And not surprisingly, the new organization is a very pleasant place in which to work.

The process of discovering this new system environment is what this book is about. The participants in the story discover a new way of looking at business and the measurements of success. The process takes lessons from the Japanese, Henry Ford, Frederick W. Taylor, and many others. But the lessons are intended to lead the participants and the reader on a discovery of the new organization.

On a grand scale, it can be said that this process allows all members of the organization to discover improvements in the work, which pays for the changing process as it progresses. The employees discover that changes occur very quickly when everyone has the same focus. Managers and workers alike see profit for what it really is—the lifeblood of the company. They discover that it is not only OK to talk about profits, it's necessary.

As the discovery process progresses, several crucial issues are exposed.

1. Technology is not the answer to America's problems. It is part of the equation, but it must be balanced with an efficient use of all the assets, including the people, of the corporation. This book provides an alternative measure of this efficiency, and terms it profitability. In the context of this book, profitability is defined as an equation: profit divided by the efficient use of the assets necessary to create that profit. It opens up interesting discussions about measures of success.
2. Companies need better measures of how they are doing in managing the business. The discovery process opens up several alternatives for consideration: profitability is certainly one. But the measurements must be timely, and that is critical to the success of any measurement program. They must also be visible and available to all in a non-blaming atmosphere.
3. Management needs to rethink the organization structures that have been used in the past to manage people. Something new is required. The discovery process uncovers a technique for showing managers the way to a different change process that is focused on understanding the right work of the organization. The right work will lead to the right organization.
4. Managers need a new perspective on what is possible. This discovery process leads to very rapid implementation. The results are seen in the early weeks of the process so that ongoing expenses are covered by improved performance in the organization. As the organization changes, the employees learn what works and what doesn't. Change with other methods is commonly so slow because we aren't going about it correctly.
5. We need to re-examine our means of training. Discovery uses a different methodology to transfer information to participants in the program. As real problems are introduced by the employees, different techniques are introduced only as they are required to analyze and scope the problem. This differs from alternative methodologies that teach techniques in a train-the-trainer program. Two problems are introduced with this approach: students may learn techniques that they never use, and then determine that the class is a waste of time; the trainers themselves may be the problem in the organization.

As the discovery proceeds, there is an underlying theme of the process: No Blame. This allows the participants to introduce contrary ideas and observations without negative consequences. Without this condition, people are reluctant to introduce an idea or a suggestion that might jeopardize their job. No Blame eliminates that risk and expedites the change process.

A number of people have asked if this book is about a Total Quality Management Program. This isn't a TQM program. It gets the desired results, but goes about it by an entirely different method.

Acknowledgments

A number of people have contributed to this book both directly and indirectly. Mr. George Sibbald and Dr. Michael Mitchell were early contributors to the thinking that went into this manuscript. George and I have argued extensively about the different processes that exist in the VAP program. We continue to argue the merits of various approaches to the delivery of the program.

Mike has been a good friend and partner over the last several years. His contributions are everywhere in my thinking about this process and I have enjoyed his pointed suggestions for improvement of the story and content of the book. Mike and I have enjoyed the opportunities of experimenting with new ideas for delivering this program where possible.

Bill Quan, David Sato, Beth Shipka and Tom DeBettencourt have been excellent facilitators in proving that this process works in many different businesses. And we have all learned that the process continues to expose course corrections that need to be made in order for change to be sustained. Dr. Robert Zelman reviewed early drafts and helped shape the form of the storyline. And I would like to thank my office staff: my son, Lenny Bertain, Rutherford Wilson and David Kircher. All of these people had input to both story line and suggested improvements.

I have had a number of early guinea pigs who trusted my judgment enough to allow me to test my theories on their organizations. Jim Henderson of Advanced Machine Programming, San Jose, CA, Larry Lista of East Bay Generator, Oakland, CA, Paul Bergeron of Pilgrim Fireplace Equipment, Richmond, CA, Mike Bardon of General Grinding, Oakland CA, Bob Schwartz of United Plastics, Oakland, CA, Pat Perrin of Perrin Manufacturing, City of Industry, CA, Paul Rajewski of MicroAge Computers Centers of Cerritos, CA, Henry Khalife of MicroAge Computer Centers of Santa Monica, CA, Shel Milligan of California Equipment Co., Oakland, CA, and many others.

I would especially like to thank the Employment Training Panel of the State of California and particular thanks to Mr. James Quillin of the International Association of Machinists, Panel Member, and Mr. Gerry Geismar, Executive Director and Mr. Carlos Lopez, Assistant

Director for supporting my efforts to make this process available to small businesses in the State of California.

I would like to thank Les Ross and Bob Miner for their early input to this program over seven years ago. And finally, I would like to also thank Eli Goldratt for encouraging other writers to use his format of storytelling as a way of delivering ideas to a wide business readership.

1

"There is no panacea. We must ensure that business basics are completely understood and applied first, then build our businesses using selective, carefully applied, and justified technology. We must learn to capitalize on the strengths of all employees."

George Sibbald, Associate and Friend
Speech, 1989

The phone rang abruptly at 2:30 in the morning. I bolted up and grabbed it. Across the hall, in his room, the baby stirred and then whimpered with the interruption of his sleep. My wife was alarmed by this disturbance and sat up in a daze. She brushed the sand from her eyes and watched me answer the phone. It was my father and he had bad news.

My friend Charlie had just been killed in an automobile crash after a heavy bout with the bottle. According to the Highway Patrol he had hit a tree near our old drinking establishment. He died shortly after arriving at the hospital.

Charlie and I had worked at Osgood's—a local manufacturing company—as machinists, and life was pretty good. We hunted together and fished every lake and stream within 300 miles of our homes. Although he was closer to my father's age, Charlie had become my friend at work and at play.

Our lives changed when Osgood's closed. Charlie and I were out of work and that was a miserable experience. My wife Sandy was pregnant at the time, and having a baby while your husband is unemployed is not a prospect for happiness. We were barely surviving.

Depressed, I hung up the phone. What was I going to say to Phyllis, Charlie's wife? Words really never cut it. I got up and pulled on my clothes. The irony of Charlie's death was that today I was starting a new job and Charlie wasn't. Charlie had been turned down for a job that I got.

I put a pot of coffee on and the phone rang again. It was Phyllis, telling me what had happened. I told her that my father had called moments earlier. As I was talking she began to cry. I comforted her as best I could. She'd called to tell me what Charlie had said to her just before he died.

She had met the ambulance at the hospital, and just before Charlie died, he told her that I was to get his tools because I was the son he never had. She went on: "Charlie told me that you were the best friend he had. And you know what else he said? He told me to call you and wish you well on the new job."

She did what he asked and told me to go back to bed. "Charlie would want you to give it your best in the morning," she said. "I know you will miss him but you need to take care of your family first. Stop by after work and tell me how it went."

I turned the coffee pot off, got undressed and went back to bed. I couldn't sleep but I dozed a bit. Why was life so unfair?

Morning arrived quickly. I got up and got dressed again. The new job was 40 miles away and I had to get up early to make it on time. I was anxious to get to work and I couldn't be late. I went downstairs to go warm up the truck. As I headed out the kitchen door I noticed that it was raining. My coat was missing from the clothes rack next to the back porch entrance, and I was going to get soaked.

Buddy, my 10-year-old son, loved to wear my coat. Whenever he did, he forgot to put it away. I was angry at him for a moment but then I remembered that he was still a little boy. I had the feeling that my first day on the job was going to be an awful day.

I headed out to the driveway and opened the door of my truck. It was chilly in the old Dodge pickup as I climbed into the cab. I pumped the gas a couple of times and hit the starter. The battery strained, the engine turned and the motor gradually came to life. It ran ragged because it needed a tune-up, but the money just wasn't there since I lost my job at Osgood's. Both the defroster and heater were slow coming to life on these cold mornings. I turned them both on and headed back to the house. As I rushed up the back steps, I could see the sun rising in the distance.

I opened the door and walked into the kitchen. Sandy had poured two cups of coffee. She was in her bathrobe, holding Mickey under her arm. He was born just after I had been laid off. He was a real load for Sandy to carry. Now Mickey was smiling and giggling at Sandy. He looked like a cherub in her arms.

Sandy hated mornings but tried to get up and see me out the door. It had been tough on her over the last several months. As she held

Mickey, he began to squirm and reach in my direction. I grabbed him and gave him a big hug.

Buddy was stirring in another room. He heard us talking and realized that I was about to head out the door for my first day on the new job. Kids know when events are important to their parents. Buddy sure knew. He came out to breakfast with Boo, his little yellow teddy bear. Boo had been his sleeping partner for several years. I bought Boo on one of the training trips I had made when I worked at Osgood's.

The last few months had been hard. I had been laid off and Sandy had had a difficult time delivering Mickey. After he was born, Sandy went back to her old job working with her mom and dad at their travel agency. Before my layoff, the job had given her a chance to be around her parents, and the extra money helped us keep the house fixed up and buy those little things that we couldn't quite afford. After my layoff her job became a necessity.

The travel agency was in her parents' house and her mom helped her take care of the kids.

When we first got married, I knew Sandy was a terrific person. After the last several months, I realized how really great she is. It was pretty smooth sailing after we'd married. Since the layoff though, we really felt the strain. After hours of looking for work I would come home day after day feeling angry and depressed. Charlie and I had searched for jobs together and his support helped keep me going.

The country was in a serious recession and there weren't a lot of jobs for machinists. Our area had heavy unemployment. I was able to fill in on a couple of jobs here and there but nothing permanent was available. These odd jobs helped but they didn't pay the bills.

While I was looking for work, Sandy never said anything about my not working. Some of my friends were not having it so easy because their wives were on them all the time for being out of work. Sandy just gave me the words of encouragement I needed to hear. We knew everything was going to work out fine; the only problem was when.

I put down my coffee cup and gave Mickey back to Sandy. I kissed her good-bye, gave Mickey a kiss, and hugged Buddy and Boo. Buddy stood at the window and waved as I backed down the driveway.

I headed out to my first day on the new job. I was excited about this opportunity but miserable over my friend's death. This was not a great way to start a new job.

As I drove to the new plant, I thought about the past. I'd started work at Osgood Manufacturing right out of high school. I had been a reasonably good student and thought that I might go on to college, but decided not to. My dad and grandpa had both worked at Osgood's. I did well in my high school shop classes and decided to continue the family tradition at Osgood's. My dad worked for Osgood's as a machinist and he had a small shop at home where he did odd jobs in the evening and on weekends for businesses in town that needed quality machine work done. He was a good machinist and a good teacher.

As a child I would sit on the bench behind his lathe and watch him work for hours. I loved the smell of cutting oil. I was always curious about the cutting of threads. I could never understand how he turned threads on a piece of metal with such precision.

My dad was a good trainer, and taught me how to think like a machinist.

He introduced me to all of his work buddies as I was growing up. I liked to listen to them discuss various ways to make a particular part. They would sit out in Dad's shop and talk for hours as they traded different ways to work through the manufacture of a part that Dad was working on.

They never seemed to argue with each other. After hours of talking, they would finally settle on a solution and complete the part.

When I went to work at Osgood's it looked like a good deal. Osgood's had been in business for years. Jimmie, Old Man Osgood's son, had just taken over and he was expanding the plant. I joined the union and served my apprenticeship. Old Man Osgood had ordered several new computer-controlled milling machines and he wanted me to learn how to program them. I went away to computer school and didn't like it one bit. I had to spend a lot of time away from Sandy while I was learning, but the training was good because it allowed me to become a journeyman quickly.

Mr. Osgood always encouraged all of us to get training. With his help, I took some engineering and computer-aided machining courses that the local community college offered with the union.

Computers were very discouraging to me. I found out later they were discouraging to most people. I really had a hard time figuring out the best ways to write programs to make the different parts. I remember calling Osgood to tell him that I just wasn't cutting it and that he ought to get another guy to take my place. I'll never forget what he said to me: "Stick with it, son, you can do it! It may not be easy, we didn't say it would be. We need you to learn that job so we can improve our product line. Just learn what you can now. If you have to go back a second time to learn a little more, don't worry about it." He was a really supportive boss.

It was hard but I did learn how to write the programs. I also taught several other people at the plant how to run the machines. Jimmie Osgood liked my work and continually supported my efforts to train other people in the company. He bought several new machines to use with a new product line, and we were going great guns.

My dad had worked at Osgood's for thirty-seven years and was having a hard time dealing with all the new machines. He liked his old manual lathe and mill and didn't like changes, so he decided to retire. I was thirty-one and had been at Osgood's for twelve years when they gave me my dad's job. I became a foreman.

I was a foreman for a little less than a year when things got bad for all of us at Osgood's. Jimmie got killed in a car accident and the old man came back to try and run the whole operation. After Jimmie's death, Old Man Osgood was just not the same. He did what he could but it was in vain. He put the plant up for sale.

Pretty soon a group of investors from back East bought the company, and they brought in a new management team to run it. The head of the group was a hotshot from some business school who was supposed to know what was going on. He was a very impersonal guy who never talked to anyone. We called him *Darth Vader* because he drove a black BMW with dark opaque windows. When he got out of the car he always had on dark sunglasses and black gloves. He always parked his "Beamer" in the shade and covered it with a sissy cover.

Whatever he was trying to do, his management style did not go well with most of us. When he came on board, things went badly.

Charlie was a great machinist and one of my dad's friends. He was in his mid-50s and had been at Osgood's for years. Charlie was one of those old-time machinists who used all his senses. He could tell if a piece was being machined properly with enough cutting fluid just by the smell of the oil as it cooled the parts it was cutting. He knew if a part was being ground properly by the shape and color of the spark flying off the grinding wheel. Charlie was good and everyone in the shop knew it.

Charlie loved to read the machinists' magazines and brochures that the salespeople left in the lunchroom. One day he found a solution to a setup problem on the old Warner-Swasey NC machines, using a magazine article. So he came over to me and said that he figured he had a way to solve the setup problem in drilling centers on all those castings. All we had to do was buy a few more boring bars and dedicate them to specific jobs. It was a neat solution to a big problem. It would have greatly increased our production in that area because it would have reduced our setup by 30%.

After lunch Charlie and I went up to the engineering department. Before we could always go to Tom, the head of engineering, any time we wanted to discuss anything that had to do with production problems. He would take the time to listen to us. After we explained an idea to him, we would argue through several alternative approaches. The end result was usually that he would let us go ahead with our ideas.

When we arrived at engineering to see Tom we found out that he was no longer with the company. We hadn't heard that Tom was fired. A new secretary stopped us. She quizzed us on why we were in engineering and not on the shop floor.

After a few minutes of this interrogation, she buzzed someone, and a junior engineer came to find out what we were doing in the engineering department. We showed this guy the article from the tooling magazine and our cost figures to justify the expenditure. He took our information and told us that he would look over the figures and get back to us next week. He didn't even say thank you. He just headed back to his office.

Charlie and I stood there for a minute. We really felt stupid. We turned and headed out of engineering and back to the shop floor. A couple of days later, my boss came over to me and said in no uncertain terms that *"engineers* do the *engineering* and *machinists* do the *machining."* As I left he asked, "You got that?"

Yeah, I got it alright. If you want my opinion, that's what's wrong with a lot of these modern companies in America today. Engineers do the engineering, but damn it, they don't own the market on ideas. Charlie and I were pretty good, and we had good ideas.

I couldn't understand what was happening at work. Why were we being treated so badly? The new management team seemed to bring in a lot of good work. They had designed a couple of new product lines and we were producing full bore on two shifts. Immediately after the acquisition, we were very busy with a huge backlog.

After a couple of months things started to get crazy. We would work like hell to get an order out only to find we were missing a key part when we went to assemble it. Parts started to pile up everywhere. We would make a run of parts and then find out that we didn't need them right away. By the time we did need them, we had to hunt all over to find them.

The situation kept getting worse. We'd get incomplete specifications from engineering. The plant manager would say, "Look, start the run and the rest of the specs will be down by the time you need them." The specs were never on time, or if they were, the previous specs were wrong. We would machine a part and then have to do it over again because it didn't fit the matching part of the lower assembly.

The investors had taken on a big debt to buy Osgood's, so we were really scrambling to get the products out the door. It seemed that even with all the new machinery we kept falling further behind. When the old man ran the company, we would solve problems as they came up. But the new management didn't run things that way. I would take a problem to the superintendent and he'd send it up to Engineering. A couple of days later new drawings would come down and we'd try to make them work.

It was clear that the company was in trouble. Morale in the shop began to slide. Some of the workers found other jobs. Even Charlie seemed to get worn down. He just did what he was told. He ran the machine and he didn't even bother to tell them the parts were screwed up. He didn't pick up the machining magazines anymore.

We started having trouble between the union and management because management was trying to change the work rules. Management wanted the machinists to set up the machines and to have helpers run them. It was just one more hassle.

It was getting pretty hard for me to get up to go to work. I hung in there because I felt like that's where I belonged. My father taught me that when you work for someone you give them your best, and I really tried to do that.

After a while under the new management getting up in the morning wasn't a problem anymore because they closed the plant. They said that the union wages were too high and that with the restrictive work rules they couldn't compete. A bunch of lowboy trailers were pulled into the lot by Mack tractors and the machinery was carted off to parts unknown. The local paper did a front page story about why the plant closed and said that the machinery was being shipped to a facility in Mexico.

Things became tough after the closure. A few years before, with help from my folks and my in-laws, Sandy and I had been able to buy a couple of acres outside of town that had a nice little house on it. The bank held our mortgage, but it was a payment that we could easily handle on my wages. The plant closing made our life miserable. We used up our savings after several months. Sandy's mom and dad and my parents helped us as much as they could.

I had to file for unemployment. I hated waiting in lines. The state people were no help. When I submitted my form for enrollment, I made a mistake. I put the wrong date on a line and had to go back again to get it right.

There was an old lady running the show who was really terrible. She acted like everybody in the unemployment line was taking *her* money. To punish me for my mistake in filling out the form, she delayed the payment of my benefits by two weeks.

As soon as I was laid off, I went down to the union hall. It was just like going to work, I saw all the same faces. Some of the people found jobs pretty quickly, but with 115 machinists unemployed all at once, the market was soon saturated.

Charlie and I looked for work together so that we could share gas and leads. We followed up every possible lead that we got. When we had been turned down by all the companies in a ten-mile radius from home, we expanded our search by moving in an ever-widening circle.

One afternoon, before Charlie and I were finished, he pulled a pint of whiskey from his coat pocket. He removed the top, took a long swig and offered it to me. This really pissed me off. I was depressed about not finding work and I didn't need alcohol. I told him, "Goddamnit, Charlie, nobody's gonna hire us if you smell like booze."

I should have seen it coming when Charlie responded: "Nobody's gonna hire an old man like me anyway, so what's the difference?"

I was unwilling to give up. I said, "Charlie, remember when you used to come over to Dad's place on Saturday? I sure do. You really helped him out a lot in those days. You're the best. And you know it. You've forgotten more about machine work than most guys will ever know. If you just hang in there, it'll be alright." He didn't say anything, he just took another swig and stared off into space.

The next morning when I picked Charlie up, he actually looked pretty good as he lumbered across the lawn. He jumped into the truck and said, "Thanks for your support yesterday. I needed that. I tossed the pint." I was feeling pretty good when we pulled into the parking lot at Quality Pump. We went into the personnel department and filled out employment applications for the umpteenth time. They all looked the same, asked the same questions, and required signatures in the same location. *What a waste!*

I submitted the form to the woman at the front desk. After a while the receptionist called Charlie and he went in for an interview. In a few minutes he came out with a little smile on his face and whispered to me, "The guy said they're getting ready to put some people on!"

I was called in a few minutes later. The guy on the other side of the desk looked at my application and said that he might be able to use me. He thanked me for coming and said that he would let me know. All the way home, Charlie remained pretty excited. This was the best prospect we'd had in a long time.

I went right home after I dropped Charlie off. As I pulled into the driveway, Buddy was there with his glove and bat. I got out of the truck, kissed Buddy and went into the house to see Sandy. She was walking over to pick up the phone. She answered it as I picked up Mickey and Cathy. Cathy is our four-year-old beauty. She looks just like her mother. She never could get up to see me off in the morning, she deferred that responsibility to Buddy. At night she insisted that I was her exclusive territory.

I tried to pay attention to Cathy but Sandy signaled that the phone was for me. It was the personnel manager where we had interviewed asking me if I could start in the morning. Of course I told him yes immediately. I then asked about Charlie. The personnel manager said that he was sorry, but that they couldn't use him.

About nine o'clock Charlie called and spoke with Sandy. She told him that I was going to work. He didn't say anything and just hung up the phone.

I turned up the volume on my favorite country station, KPAY, ". . . you provide the city, we provide the country, a little bit of country in the city." Johnny Paycheck began singing, "Take this job and shove it, I ain't a'workin' here no more." I started laughing when I sang along because I really didn't know whether or not I wanted to shove my job; I hadn't even started to work.

When I got there, I parked my truck and went into the office. I filled out all the required paperwork. A couple of the other guys filling out paperwork had worked with me at Osgood's. We waited just a short time until this huge guy walked into the office. The personnel director pointed us out as the new hires and he led us to the shop floor. As we walked, he pulled the stub of a cigar from the pocket of his overalls, lit it and introduced himself as Jack, the plant superintendent.

Jack must have been six foot five or six and he weighed at least three hundred fifty pounds. Everyone seemed to like him and he laughed and joked with people as he walked around. He showed us around the plant. He took us to the tool crib and left me there with Billy, one of his foremen. Billy led me over to a small computer-controlled milling machine and asked, "You ever run one of these before?"

I told him that I had and he pulled a drawing from his clipboard, pointed to a pallet with some rough stock on it and said, "Here's the stock, and this is what we need to make. You'll find all the tools you need in the tool crib. Go to work."

My first job was pretty simple. I was able to set it up and start running it in about three hours. Billy came by just as I was finishing up and he seemed pleased. He put me with another guy doing setup for another job and left. As I punched out that afternoon, Jack came up and said, "Good day, young man, you're going to work just fine."

After work I stopped by to see Phyllis and told her about the new job. She listened for a while but every time she looked at me she cried. I reminded her of Charlie and she couldn't contain herself. I stayed a little while longer, then got up to leave and she gave me a big hug. Another friend arrived to comfort Phyllis as I headed for home.

The next morning I completed the job I had started the previous afternoon. The guy I was working with was the lead man from the tool and die shop. His name was Gus and he had been at this plant for a long time. He was a good enough hand, but he seemed too cocky. He was not as good as Charlie. He bragged that he and his crew were the only ones in the plant who knew what was going on besides Jack. He said, "That Jack's a clever bastard."

I liked working at the new plant. The group of guys was good, but I couldn't help noticing that this plant looked an awful lot like Osgood's before it closed down. There were pallets of WIP (work in process) everywhere.

Products seemed to get out in time, but there was always a lot of rescheduling going on. Everyone was putting in lots of overtime and no one seemed to mind because they were making pretty good money.

I quickly got the feeling that the same things were happening here that happened at Osgood's. Just as I'd get a job setup, I'd be told to tear it down and start another one.

Jack was in charge. There was no denying that. He ran the department like it was his own personal kingdom. Jack seemed to like my work, so he never gave me any trouble, but whenever he got the chance, he would terrorize the foremen just to let them know who was boss.

On my third day, Gus and I were doing a setup for another rush job. Jack was overseeing the work, sending people scurrying around to get us whatever we needed so that we could get the job running. At that moment the General Manager and the head of Sales walked over to him. The G.M. started to get on Jack's case about the order being late, and Jack blew up. He started yelling that they didn't know his problems, that he couldn't get reliable suppliers and that these old machines couldn't be expected to keep up with all the orders. Jack only knew one way to manage. He yelled, but he never listened.

While he was yelling, Jack was waving his arms. He began backing these two guys toward the offices. Finally, the two Executives were at the door of the office, and when the Sales Vice President opened it, they beat a hasty retreat.

Gus began laughing like hell while this was going on. "That damned Jack, he doesn't take crap from nobody. He's got that G.M. scared of his own shadow." Even though Gus seemed to think it was the funniest thing he'd ever seen, I started getting a little nervous. I had just gone through one plant closure and was not looking forward to another.

In a way, Charlie got off easy. He was out of this rat race and here I was back in the middle of another crazy deal. Jack and Charlie had gone to school together, so Jack had no problem letting me off to go to the funeral. I went into work early to help get the job that I was working on completed. On the way to the funeral, I stopped and picked up Sandy and we met my mom and dad at the church. There were a lot of people from Osgood's there. Even Old Man Osgood showed up. He looked like he'd aged twenty years since I'd last seen him.

After the burial, a few of us from the old plant went down to see where the accident had happened. You could see the plant from where we were and one of the guys noticed that the "For Sale" sign was gone.

Shirley, one of the gals who had worked in my department, called her brother who owned the local real estate office. She came back with tears in her eyes and said, "They're going to tear down the plant and put up a shopping mall! They're going to put a damn McDonald's right there on the corner!"

I thought, Great! Some kid will be flipping hamburgers where we used to turn metal. That's America for you. Tear down a factory and put up another fast food joint.

The next morning when Gus and I arrived the plant was completely clean! All the pallets of WIP were gone.

When I asked Gus about it he said, "I told you Jack was clever. We're doing physical inventory. The auditors start tomorrow. Jack took most of the WIP and stashed it in that old warehouse out back. He's been doing it for years. You see, we have to pay a higher tax on WIP than on stock, so Jack hides it back there and calls it raw material. The guys over in accounting don't have a clue what's going on. They just know we look real good at tax time and that makes Jack look like a hero."

Soon afterward it really hit the fan. The auditors looked in the warehouse and found the WIP. The plant was closed down for a couple of days while the big guns from the company's accounting firm sent an army of auditors into the plant. When we came back to work, Jack was gone.

For a couple of weeks we sort of stumbled around, with the general manager and the foremen trying to run things. Then we got a new plant manager. He met with us and said his name was Jim. He told us that the last plant where he worked had just closed down. He said that he was glad to have a job and hoped to make some changes in the plant so that we'd become more efficient.

The last thing he said was that everybody was going to keep their jobs, that nobody would be laid off. That made me feel better because I had been one of the last hires, so I would probably be one of the first to go.

Jim came over to my station after the meeting and said he was sorry about Charlie; he had known him and he had also known that he was a good hand.

Jim meant what he said about changes. The first thing he did was move his desk onto the shop floor. He had some carpenters come in and knock out the wall between his old office and several other offices that were only being used for storage. The room was now big enough to easily hold twenty or thirty people. He brought in some tables and chairs, a VCR and a TV. He also got an overhead projector and put up several blackboards. He was making changes alright, but I couldn't see how watching TV was going to make us more efficient.

One afternoon, about a week after the carpenters finished, Jim came walking through the shop with an interesting-looking guy. He and Jim were watching things and stopping here and there to talk with some of the workers. They came over to my station and Jim said, "This is Dr. Elbie. He's going to help us make some of the changes that I talked about."

Elbie had a good firm handshake, and said that he looked forward to working with us. He didn't look like he could help much with machine work. He was in his mid-forties and was dressed in slacks and a sports coat. He wore metal-rimmed glasses and a wild pink pullover shirt. He wasn't real tall but he looked strong. Not like a bodybuilder, but like a swimmer or someone who grew up on a farm. I figured, Let's see what this Dr. Elbie can do.

2

Things at Quality Pump started to get a little better after Jim came on board. Jim came up with some new scheduling guidelines that really cut down on our lead time. The piles of WIP started to get smaller and it seemed to me that I was getting a little more done each day. Then Dr. Elbie started coming by two or three times a week to spend the afternoon just looking at equipment, or talking with the workers in various departments.

One afternoon Dr. Elbie was down at the tool and die department talking with Gus and his crew. Dr. Elbie must have made a joke, because everyone was laughing and pointing at Gus. Pretty soon Gus came over to me and said, "Hey, you want to hear a good one? This guy, Dr. Elbie, says we can probably reduce our average setup time from four hours to fifteen minutes. And," Gus paused, "you know what else he said?"

It seemed crazy to me and I just answered, "I have no idea."

Gus went on, "He said that we could probably accomplish this *miracle* in less than six months and not spend more than fifteen thousand dollars." Then he said, "You know what that new room is for? It's a damn classroom! They want to send us all to school. They want to train everyone. Jim seems to think it will help the company save some money."

Jim told me earlier that setup accounted for over 25% of the total direct labor charge in the factory. I'm sure that we weren't any better at Osgood's. Jim said that Dr. Elbie felt that a reasonable target for setup was no more than 5% of the total direct labor charge. To me that seemed insane.

Then Gus explained, "My God! Where do they ever find these guys? If it isn't this, it's Quality Circles. If it isn't Quality Circles, it's some other 'feel good' crap. Anyway, Elbie will be over here in a few minutes, so humor him."

It didn't make any sense. Setup, or change over, is one part of the business that Gus and his guys really knew. They had been doing the layouts of new jobs in the factory for over thirty years, but we needed to change something. I knew that Gus and his crew were good but

Uncle Jerry used to say that people with experience usually have the wrong experiences.

In this case, how could this Dr. Elbie know more about setups in this plant than Gus and his crew? This wasn't making any sense. If Jim wanted to improve the factory, why didn't he do what managers always do—just buy some new machines to increase our productivity? But my dad had told me a million times: Machines rarely solve productivity problems! People do!

From reading some of the tool and machine magazines, I knew that there were a lot of new tools that we could buy to improve our operation. Every time I mentioned them in any of our discussions, Jim told me to think of other ways to do our manufacturing.

Gus left and Dr. Elbie went over to Jim's desk. They were talking and looking over in my direction. I put my head down and kept working. Suddenly, I noticed Dr. Elbie standing on the other side of my workbench looking over at the computer-controlled turning center in the next work area. It was kind of spooky, he just appeared there. As I looked his way, he asked, "How long did this last setup take?"

After thinking it over I said that I started after yesterday afternoon's break and finished just before noon today. The first unit produced on my machine (we call it the "first article") passed inspection. Right after lunch I started producing parts for the job. "About seven hours," I told Dr. Elbie.

He looked at me for a few minutes and asked me if I thought it would be crazy to reduce that time by 50%. I replied, "Do you mean to ask me if we could do a complete setup for this job in three and a half hours? Absolutely not! This is one of the toughest jobs that we do around here. I've only been doing this setup for a little while, but I don't see how to reduce it any further."

Dr. Elbie started to explain when Jim came over and asked me how everything was going. "Well, Jim," I said, "Dr. Elbie just asked me an interesting question."

"What was that?" Jim asked.

"He wanted to know if I thought that this setup time could be cut in half."

"And what was your response?" Jim asked.

I replied, "Well, I don't know much about this particular setup, but one thing I do know is that Gus and his guys have done a pretty good job of designing the fixtures and jigs for this job. I don't see how we can save much more time without buying some new machinery."

The following Monday morning I drove into the parking lot at Quality and parked. I joined some people who were walking toward the plant entrance. We had to wait at the driveway because Mr. Grimes was just pulling in. It was unusual for Mr. Grimes, the owner of Quality Pump, to be there so early. He swung his Mercedes into his reserved space and got out of the car.

Jim and Dr. Elbie had been standing near Jim's car, and now they went to greet Mr. Grimes. Mr. Grimes and Dr. Elbie shook hands and the three men walked over to the offices.

I punched in and went over to my station to start a setup. After a few minutes Gus came over with the tooling I needed and we worked together setting up the run. Gus said, "Did you see the old man come in early today? Something must be up. Everyone knows that a company is really in trouble when the president gets there early!"

I told him that I'd seen Mr. Grimes, Dr. Elbie and Jim walk into the office. Gus and I finished the setup and I started the job. Gus went over to some of his other people and began to work with them.

After about half an hour, Mr. Grimes, Dr. Elbie and Jim came out to the shop floor. They went into the classroom and Dr. Elbie pulled a videotape from his briefcase. They watched the video for about fifteen minutes and then started walking toward my machine. As they approached, I could see that Dr. Elbie had a binder with a sheaf of papers sticking out of it.

Dr. Elbie pointed to the programming computer on my machine and then showed Mr. Grimes a diagram. Mr. Grimes asked him a question and he pointed to a pallet of WIP near my machine. That was my next job. Mr. Grimes came over to me and asked, "Do you think we can reduce setup time like Dr. Elbie says?"

I said, "I don't think so, but I'll have to reserve my judgment until we see the results of his setup reduction program. I think our own guys are pretty good but Jim asked me to work with Dr. Elbie and see what happens. According to Jim, what Dr. Elbie says is good for us, but Gus and his people seem to have a pretty good handle on how to set this stuff up. I'm not so sure they'll listen to Dr. Elbie."

Mr. Grimes turned to Dr. Elbie, "Don't worry—I'll get Gus to come around." He shook Dr. Elbie's hand and said "Look's like we've got a deal."

Dr. Elbie said, "Great, we'll start class next Monday."

3

On Thursday morning Dr. Elbie walked to Jim's desk in a hurry. He had a computer printout in his hand and he looked angry. He said, "Jim, what is this crap? We're trying to help this business and we need to train everybody. This printout shows that only the foremen are scheduled for training!" The whole shop got quiet because everyone could hear Dr. Elbie yelling at Jim.

Jim came around his desk and looked at the printout Dr. Elbie was holding and said, "I don't know why everyone's not listed. I'll give Grimes a call and see if I can find out."

Jim made the call and Mr. Grimes approached his desk a few minutes later. Dr. Elbie held the printout and pointed to it as he spoke with Mr. Grimes. Mr. Grimes listened for a minute and then he started to get red in the face. I don't know what was said but both of them seemed to get pretty hot. Jim got between them and pointed toward the classroom, and Dr. Elbie and Mr. Grimes went in there and shut the door. After about ten minutes, Dr. Elbie and Mr. Grimes came out of the classroom. Mr. Grimes went back to his office and Dr. Elbie went over to Jim's desk and spoke with him, then left.

As I worked, I tried to figure out what might have happened between Mr. Grimes and Dr. Elbie. Jim glanced over in my direction and I quickly looked away. Jim walked slowly over to my area. His head was down a bit. He tapped me on the shoulder and asked almost sheepishly, "I guess you saw that?"

"As a matter of fact, yes, I did. What's going on?"

"Well," Jim said, "this plant isn't doing any better than your old factory at Osgood's. Mr. Grimes was initially enthusiastic about doing the training, but he had second thoughts, so he changed the scheduling. Just now he told Dr. Elbie that they couldn't afford to do all the training, and that he was cancelling most of the training program except for a pilot group of managers. Dr. Elbie came out to tell me the news. As you could see, he's not pleased."

Just then, Dr. Elbie appeared at Jim's elbow. He tapped Jim on the shoulder and said, "Jim, I'm sorry for getting so mad. Mr. Grimes is so typical of many American executives that I have met. He can't break loose from the idea that training people is a cost. I tried to explain to him that his people were an undeclared asset of the corporation, and training the people only increases the value of that asset. He insisted that the recent quarter's results don't give him any room to do training. The bankers want immediate results on the company's loan obligation or they may have to take some action.

"I really shouldn't be talking about this with you here," Dr. Elbie said to me, "but as far as I'm concerned there is no reason that the workers shouldn't know what is guiding the thinking of management. What the hell do I have to do to convince him? It just pisses me off."

I hadn't heard Dr. Elbie use any foul language before. He was beginning to sound like one of us. Dr. Elbie grabbed Jim by the elbow and led him away. As they left, I heard Dr. Elbie say, "I've one ace to play, and now's the time to play it."

They both headed to the front offices. I expected them to meet with Mr. Grimes. I went back to my job and got the spindle turning.

About an hour later I saw Jim heading out to my area with Mr. Grimes, Dr. Elbie and the president of our union local, Ed Daley. Dr. Elbie was holding the piece of paper with the times from my last setup in front of Mr. Grimes. He was telling him, ". . . and like I told you in your office, you're focusing on the wrong issue. If you focus on profit alone, you're going to make the wrong decision. You have to focus on profitability."

I was having a difficult time following much of the discussion because they were talking about financial stuff, which I don't understand. Dr. Elbie went over to the shop blackboard and started writing as he was talking. He wrote:

$$\text{Profitability} = \frac{\text{Profit}}{\text{Efficient Use of Assets}}$$

Then he said, "By using this definition you can get a handle on the measure of operating efficiency. And by efficient use of assets, I mean the sum total of all the assets that are used to generate those profits: equipment, inventory, accounts receivable, and other current assets and your people.

"We can then write the profitability formula as follows:"

The New Turnaround

$$\text{Productivity} = \frac{\text{Revenue} - \text{Costs}}{\underline{\text{Wastes} + \text{Building \& Equipment} + \text{Inventory} + \text{A/R} + \text{Cash}}}$$
$$\text{Efficiency of Use}$$

"And by waste, I mean everything that you do in the system that doesn't add value. We will discuss this in detail in the class. But you must look beyond the profit equations. You and the cost accountants have said that you can't afford to spend any time on training. You currently spend about 35% of your shop time on setups; I'm telling you that you can't afford not to bring that number under control.

"In order to make your whole shop more efficient and profitable we need to look at the rate at which you convert raw materials to cash. If you do, then you have a real formula for success. You can't look at profits alone. You need to look at all the items that contribute to improved profitability, which includes the rate at which you convert ideas and raw materials to cash and the elimination of waste in your operations. That will be an integral part of the training program: *to teach these principles to your employees.*"

Dr. Elbie stopped for a second and waited for Mr. Grimes to respond, but he didn't. He just stood there. Finally, Mr. Grimes said, "From what you just showed me and from last quarter's figures I can see that I really have no choice! I'm still the major stockholder and I want to see those profits, so let's get started!"

Dr. Elbie responded, "Great! I'll be here Monday morning to start the training. There will be six classes of twenty people per class. The first class will start at seven o'clock and go for one hour. There will be a half-hour break between each class. The schedule will look like this:

First Class	7:00–8:00
Second Class	8:30–9:30
Third Class	10:00–11:00
Fourth Class	1:00–2:00
Fifth Class	2:30–3:30
Sixth Class	4:00–5:00

That will get all one hundred twenty employees in the training. We'll have a meeting of all your managers and supervisors tomorrow to go over the agenda. Everyone will be attending these sessions. Right?"

"Well, not really," Mr. Grimes responded. "Roland Diamond, the head of sales, doesn't think that the sales people will have time to attend because they'll be out selling. Our sales have been down and we need everyone out in the field. As you said earlier, we have to increase profitability and one way we can do that is to increase revenues. Right?"

Dr. Elbie shot back, "You haven't been listening to anything that I have been telling you. We are trying to create a new team in your company. Everyone's on the team, not just factory people or finance people, even sales people are part of the team.

"There are no excuses. Have them attend the first session in the morning or the last one in the evening. They absolutely have to be there!"

Then he said, "By the way, you're right, you do need to increase sales, and after one week in these classes your sales people will be so excited about the impending improvement possibilities that they'll have all the motivation in the world. You have to be there too.

"If you don't show up, everyone will get the wrong idea that this is a neat little exercise and Mr. Grimes doesn't care. If you don't attend, the sessions will become meaningless. Mr. Diamond will be just as excited as you. What do you think his sales would be if you reduced your lead time from twelve weeks to one week? When he sees that possibility, he will get on board. Just be there for the first day's classes to show your interest."

Dr. Elbie then turned to Jim. "That was the reason that the process was so slow over at Prescott's. Jack Prescott didn't attend the early sessions. As soon as he started attending the sessions, the program really kicked into high gear.

"You know Prescott's, don't you, Mr. Grimes? I did this training over there with several of my associates. In the first four weeks his people came up with all kinds of good ideas. We spent those first few weeks identifying specific forms of waste in the business. As I recall during the first four days, each of the six classes identified at least sixty major wastes in the company and one class alone identified ninety-five wastes. When all the wastes were separated and sized, the total value of the waste in the business was over six million dollars!

"That isn't a poor reflection of Prescott's. It's actually very typical of what we find in almost every company. If there are two classes or ten classes, we always identify an average of one million dollars of waste per class.

"Mr. Grimes, remember what I told you the other day. We use $25 per hour to size the time component of waste. $25 per hour is supposed to represent the cost of keeping an employee paid and covering the overhead.

"You'll agree that the number is low, but when all the wastes are calculated, even at $25 an hour, the amount of waste is still significant. Do you agree with me that the number is low?"

John Grimes looked at Dr. Elbie for a little while and then stared off in space for a few seconds and said, "You know what my number really is? I think it's over $62 per hour. If I understand you right, you are interested in the total costs to break even, say, on a month-to-month basis, divided by the total number of hours worked by everyone that month. You know, Elbie, $25 an hour *is* on the low side."

"You've got it, John," Dr. Elbie said. "I use $25 per hour to simplify the calculations. If I used the real numbers no one would believe them anyway. Even at $25 per hour, all wastes can be readily compared and priorities can be established. We normally go about sizing the wastes in the second week of the class and try to figure out how many hours per day or week are attributed to each particular waste. Then we quantify the waste on a yearly basis and rank how difficult it is to fix the particular waste. We calculate waste as a yearly number because we want to compare it to profit, which is calculated on a yearly basis.

"If you disagree with the size of a particular waste, you will tell me that the hours of waste identified are high by 50%. I would then double the hourly cost to get closer to the real number rate, and the size of the waste remains the same. Even $50 per hour is on the low side for most companies. As you pointed out a few minutes ago, it's even low for your company. I defend the class numbers because we size the waste by class consensus and the employees usually have a pretty good feel for the size of the problem. We'll get into this during the first week and you'll be surprised at some of the issues that get raised in the discussions.

"One of the more interesting issues that I want you to watch is your net productivity. We will begin training and take your people off the production lines for five hours per week. During that time you'll have 12.5% fewer hours of production, but you won't lose that much total production. In fact, you'll probably only lose about 3% or 4% of the current production capacity."

I was struck by several things as Dr. Elbie was talking. First, Mr. Grimes was really paying attention to him. I had heard from several of the guys that Mr. Grimes was usually pretty standoffish. He never normally listened to anyone.

I wondered how Dr. Elbie could say up front that there will be one million dollars of waste found by each class. That was a really big number. Could the company be that bad? Was he also saying that he could find that much waste in any company? I wondered if all American companies were in that much trouble.

The third thing that really hit home was that Dr. Elbie said we'll be losing over 12% of our production time and he doesn't believe that there will be any significant loss in production. How could he say that?

Dr. Elbie continued, ". . . and furthermore, Mr. Grimes, do you know why you won't lose the production?"

Mr. Grimes didn't want to seem ignorant but at the same time you could tell that he didn't have a clue. Jim was standing in the back with his arms folded and a little smile on his face. He obviously knew something that Mr. Grimes didn't or else he was enjoying watching Mr. Grimes squirm for a moment. There was a long pause in the conversation while Dr. Elbie waited for a response. When it was clear that none would be forthcoming, Dr. Elbie went on, "Do you ever recall reading about the Hawthorne effect?"

Again, Mr. Grimes had no response. Dr. Elbie continued, "A test was run back in the early thirties to see the effect of lighting intensity on worker productivity. In a particular plant, the lighting level was set at a very low intensity. The productivity was measured. As the lighting level increased, so did productivity. The productivity continued until the lights were at their brightest intensity. Productivity went up with light intensity. Then a curious thing happened. As they dropped the lighting intensity the productivity continued to rise. As it turned out, the productivity increased every time there was a noticeable change in the lighting intensity—whether it went up or down.

"They discovered that there was no absolute relationship between productivity and an optimum lighting level. What really mattered was that the workers felt that management was paying attention to them. Their adjustments to the lighting motivated the workers to do more.

"The same is true when training employees. I'm not talking about manipulating your people by training them. I'm talking about paying attention to them. In this program, the workers get very enthusiastic about the opportunities to help. They really do care about their work. If the company cares about them enough to take them off the lines to train them, then they'll get the work out."

I thought about that for a minute. I work about as hard as I can in my eight-hour shift and I can't get any . . . well, Dr. Elbie told me that if I worked smarter, then maybe I could get more work done. As he was talking, I began thinking about different wastes in the company. I wasn't sure what he meant by wastes. He thought that setup time was a waste. If 35% of my time is spent on setup and if Dr. Elbie showed me that I could reduce my setup by almost half, then on that basis alone I would get 17.5% more productive work done.

"And the key to this whole process," Dr. Elbie concluded, "is to get more profitable work done." I guess he answered my question.

He said, "As you'll find out, Mr. Grimes, your people will come up with some pretty good ideas that can be implemented very quickly, but you have to support the whole process to get the maximum return from this training.

"We'll need a meeting of all the managers and supervisors tomorrow morning at this management session. Your attendance will also be required, Mr. Grimes. The meeting will last three hours. We need to get the commitment and support of these people in order for the program to work. They're the first and second-line supervisors, this process of change is going to affect them the most.

"That's why we'll have this meeting. Most of these managers and supervisors will be supportive of what we are doing, some will not. Mr. Grimes, we'll need you to help get those reluctant people motivated at the meeting tomorrow and again on Monday by your presence at these first training sessions. This is very important. As I said before, if you don't show up, one or two of the managers or supervisors will interpret this as your lack of commitment to the process. If you aren't committed, the process of change that we're talking about will take a lot longer, or it may not catch on at all.

"Give Jack Prescott a call if you need any encouragement in this area. Jack didn't start his training program as a fully committed supporter but now they have regular weekly training programs for all their people."

As I listened to all this, I wondered: Do we still have enough time to fix this company before they close the doors?

4

Dr. Elbie and Jim were getting out of a car as I pulled into the parking lot on Friday morning. Jim was carrying a box from the local bakery, probably a snack for the meeting of the managers and supervisors.

I was still wondering about Dr. Elbie's suggestions on setup reduction and considering new areas for improvement. He really had me thinking.

Yesterday I figured that I could probably save some processing time by getting the programmer for my machine to change the program flow on one of the jobs. I noticed that the cutting tool speed was too slow on parts that we made out of aluminum. I could have easily doubled the speed, taken it to the maximum and still maintained quality. Over at Osgood's we always ran aluminum jobs at full machine speed. We could probably get the job done about 35% faster.

I thought that this would be a good idea to discuss with Dr. Elbie and Jim. As it was we weren't allowed to change anything: the programmer didn't talk to us, so we couldn't try anything new with him. If he talked to us it might save the company a lot of time. I wondered if setting up dumb rules created a waste.

As I headed to the factory entrance, Dr. Elbie approached me and asked, "Have you thought about our discussion the other day?"

"I haven't thought about anything else. I thought about ways we could increase production in my area. Is it alright to think of increased production and not just waste?"

"Oh, absolutely," he said. "One of the biggest wastes in the business is the waste of processing itself. You are right to look at this point positively. Instead of talking about wastes, you are talking about increasing production. It's always better to increase production by 20% than to brag about finding a million dollars worth of waste. I always like to say that the glass is half full, not half empty."

He smiled and said, "Are we having fun yet?"

I grinned and said, "I am having fun. Can I ask you a simple question? Do you think that you can really help us? I just went through one closure and from what I understand, we're in deep trouble."

"I know," Dr. Elbie replied seriously. "I know Quality Pump is in trouble, but from what I understand from some of your customers, you make a good product and lots of people want it. You must be able to satisfy their needs and twelve-week-delivery won't do that. When you have competition, you have no choice: you must be able to compete. To do that, you'll have to improve your quality and your lead time. And that's what we are going to focus on in class. Do you agree?"

"I really wouldn't know about that, but I guess Mr. Grimes does. Did he tell you that?"

"Yes, he did. In fact, he thinks that if you get your lead time down you could capture significant market share from your competition. Do you know what I mean by that?"

"Not really," I said. "I do know that we make a good product. People on the line have told me that we stand up pretty well against the competition but we take too long to fill orders and our expenses are too high. I guess all of those things are waste issues. Right?"

"After awhile everyone starts to think of me as the King of Waste. You're right though. If we get started in the class and focus on these issues of waste, we should be able to significantly affect the two issues that we mentioned: lead time and costs.

"By the way," Dr. Elbie said, "I stopped you because I understand that you have a changeover today. Could you time all the things that you are doing during the changeovers for the next week and record them on this sheet?"

He handed me a sheet of paper with a form on it. "I don't see a problem with this. What'll happen if the numbers don't get better?"

"Well, we won't shoot the messenger, if that's what you mean. We will use these numbers in the class for everyone to see. I won't be picking on you but I will be using your experiences to show everyone else in the plant that it doesn't hurt. We are not going to *blame* anyone. If the company allows you to report the facts, then we can help. We have to let you report what really happens. We need you to report honest data. That is one thing that we have to change. I have a meeting this morning with the managers and supervisors. I'll stop by your work area after the meeting and we can talk then."

After he walked away, I began to think. I realized that this was the first time that anyone in management had talked to me with respect since Old Man Osgood ran his company.

I heard from Tony that the meeting was another one of those bullshit sessions that will lead nowhere. Tony Corbelli had been on vacation for the last several weeks. In his first week back he went into a meeting where they talked about making big changes in the company! He had three years until retirement and didn't want to change anything. Boy, he was not pleased, and he let everybody know it!

I guess one of the hardest things for people to do is change. Jim told me the other day that we are all creatures of habit and change is never easy. If we don't change the way we do things in our shop we won't have any jobs to worry about.

Dr. Elbie assured me that change would happen, and people needed to be willing and able for the change to occur. Tony certainly didn't seem to be willing to change. He figured, why change anything, even if it's broken? Tony was probably going to fight any suggestions for change.

I could tell by the tone of Tony's voice that he wasn't going to enjoy these classes very much. This training was going to challenge his authority and all of our lives were going to be miserable as a result. But, if we didn't do the training, unemployment would be worse. So I figured maybe I could put up with Tony and Gus until the training ended.

I remember my father and grandfather talking about how much fun they had in their early days on the job, Grandpa in the thirties during the Depression and Dad in the sixties. Grandpa was a very skilled machinist. Mr. Osgood always listened to his machinists on how to manufacture a product. For some reason my new managers didn't want to hear ideas from workers. Maybe Dr. Elbie and Jim could change that.

5

I was in the first class on Monday morning. I could tell that this was going to be a really hot group because both Tony and Gus were there. They weren't going to let very much get by. They loved to challenge authority. In the few union meetings that I had attended, Gus and Tony were rough on the boys from the union hall.

In addition to Tony and Gus, there was Frank, a tool and die worker; Mr. Diamond, the vice president of sales; Bonnie, one of the sales people; the controller and one of his assistants; two engineers; Bernard, the head programmer; one assembly technician; two machinists; the receptionist; the blueprint shop manager; an accounts payable clerk; the head of purchasing; and Buck, the loading dock foreman, who was sitting way in the back of the classroom. The local union president, Ed Daley, was also in the room.

There were big boxes of loose-leaf binders sitting near the front of the classroom. Jim and a couple of other people were handing them out. I took mine, grabbed a seat and started leafing through it. On the cover was the word blame, and over that was a circle with a slash through it like those No Left Turn signs: *NO BLAME.*

That was a strange logo. What did it mean? Also inside were pages of graphs and formulas and occasionally pages that just had slogans on them, like "Find a simple job and do it." I looked at that big manual full of strange stuff and the TV sitting on the table in front and wondered when we'd ever have time to talk about setup.

The morning started out just as I expected. The machine shop workers all stood together and the sales people hung out loudly in the corner. Everyone else was milling around the room when Dr. Elbie and Mr. Grimes walked in. It was 7:00 A.M. right on the button.

Mr. Grimes walked to the front of the room and asked everyone to take a seat. When everyone was seated he began, "As you know, Quality Pump has been having a pretty bad time of it lately. Sales have been down, quality has been down even further and production is terrible. I know that we have all worked hard, but if we keep going the way we are, we'll lose a company and the jobs that go with it.

"I have spent a lot of time thinking about what to do. Should I sell the company to one of our competitors? Should I sell it to any number of overseas investors who want to get a foothold in the American market? Should I lay off a bunch of people and go back to being a small shop that serves only our best customers? Should I just close the plant down? Whatever option that I follow, other than improving our current operations, it'll probably lead to layoffs, and I'm unwilling to do that.

"So I'm going to invest *your time* and *my money* in a training program that I think will have a significant impact on this company. This training program has worked at companies similar to ours. In fact, if you talk with the employees at several other local companies who have completed this process, they'll tell you that it works. Not only do the companies become more profitable, they become better places to work.

"I talked with Jack Prescott, the owner of Prescott's, and he told me frankly that he wasn't so sure what he was getting into when he began this process. He had his doubts before he started the program. He wasn't sure that anything could be done to improve his operation. He was just about ready to file for bankruptcy when he met Dr. Elbie.

"Jack said that after their initial meeting, he still wasn't sure whether this training process could improve his business. He really didn't understand the process that Dr. Elbie was talking about. He didn't believe that his people could help, because he didn't see how Dr. Elbie and his team could get the improvements they said they could get from employees' ideas. But they did.

"I don't understand the process either, but I need help and I'm going to stand behind this process, support it no matter what problems come up and I'm going to wait for the results. Jack Prescott said that 'Do the training and they will come, the ideas and solutions will come.' I just hope that this process is my Field of Dreams."

A few people snickered at Mr. Grimes' little joke. He went on, "Jack Prescott also told me that I would be stupid to start this program and not give it my full commitment. And you know the reason that he

The New Turnaround

gave me? It sounded unbelievable at first, but it made sense. He said, 'This training leads to a very profitable operation. More than anything, you will find that the results happen quickly. It's very profitable and it's fast.' I liked to hear that. Those of you who know me know that I tend to be impatient."

Mr. Grimes walked over to the middle of the room, smiled and pointed his finger at us to emphasize his next point. "You know what else he said? 'Crow doesn't taste very good.' I really don't know what he meant by that but if I end up eating any during this training, you know what I'd like." He stopped, "I'd like to use some catsup."

At that point everyone laughed. Mr. Grimes continued, "I just hope that this program will help us just as much here at Quality Pump.

"Dr. Elbie is going to teach the program along with several of his associates. He calls the program VAP, which stands for the Value-added Analysis Process.

"Each class will meet every day at the same time and I'll try to attend as many classes as possible. Everyone in the company will be attending a class, every day. I will be too, unless its absolutely impossible. But all of you will be here. It's your job, just like being in the shop or in your office. Over the course of the day there will be six classes taught according to the following schedule." He handed everyone a copy of the training schedule.

"I believe that this training is really important. It is so important that I have asked the local union president, Mr. Ed Daley, to be here as well. The bottom line is we are all going to have to work together to make this company successful, and we are all going to gain from this training. The VAP training process offers management, union/labor, stockholders and customers a win-win deal. More profits mean more money for everyone. I could pocket all the increased profits but I won't do that. I want everyone to win. If we are going to turn this company around, it has to be a team effort. I really believe that, and that, my friends, is the basis of a good deal.

"Ed, would you come up here and say a few words."

At that point Ed Daley went up to the front of the classroom. He and Mr. Grimes had been at each other's throats for the last fifteen years over contract negotiations. I couldn't believe what I was seeing. They were actually smiling at each other. When Ed arrived at the front, Mr. Grimes and he shook hands, and as Mr. Grimes took a seat, Ed began to talk.

"As most of you know, John Grimes and I have had our disagreements in the past. In spite of them, we've always been able to come away from the bargaining table with a lot of respect for each other. He's always fought hard, but he's always been fair. At this time, John and I are on the same side of the table. We both support this program and we'll do everything possible to make it work.

"I have seen the results of the VAP process at Prescott's, Werner Controls, St. Clair Hospital, E & M Machining, Drums Unlimited, Executive Computers and a couple of other companies. In each case, employee involvement has dramatically improved the company's profits. In fact, I went over to an insurance company and a bank that implemented the VAP program and they got the same impressive results as the manufacturing businesses. I expect we'll see the same results here.

"I think you'll enjoy this program in the weeks ahead. Thanks again, John, for giving everyone a chance to prove themselves to you."

Mr. Grimes returned to the front and introduced Dr. Elbie. He said that Dr. Elbie had been a consultant for six years and had created the VAP process during that time.

Dr. Elbie approached the front and took off his coat. He stood over to the side as he rolled up his sleeves. His white shirt was perfectly pressed. His hair was nicely combed. I hadn't seen him look so neat in the last several weeks. I figured he was trying to impress us.

He went up to the board and wrote his name. As he turned to face the class he said, "Thank you for coming today. You can call me Jack, Dr. Elbie, just Elbie, or whatever you like. And yes, Mr. Grimes, I will provide catsup." Everyone laughed. "To begin, let me read something to you. I want you to listen carefully and see if you agree with this. It was taken from a speech given a couple of years ago by Konosuke Matsushita, the president of Matsushita Electric Company of Japan. At this point, Dr. Elbie explained that Fredrick Taylor was an early twentieth century advisor to Henry Ford, among others. Taylor is thought of as the father of the scientific approach to management. He then read the following quote very slowly and clearly for all of us to hear and understand:

> We will win and you will lose. You cannot do anything about it because your management systems are based on Taylor's principles. Worse, your heads are Taylorized too. You firmly believe that sound management means executives on one side and

workers on the other, on one side men who think and on the other side men who can only work. For you, management is the art of smoothly transferring the executives' ideas to the workers' hands.

"We have passed the Taylor stage. We are aware that business has become terribly complex. Survival is very uncertain in an environment increasingly filled with risk, the unexpected, and competition. Therefore, a company must have the constant commitment of the minds of all of its employees to survive. For us, management is the entire work force's intellectual commitment to the service of the company without self-imposed functional or class barriers.

"We have measured—better than you—the new technological and economic challenges. We know that the intelligence of a few technocrats—even the very bright ones—has become totally inadequate to face these challenges. Only the intellects of all employees can permit a company to live with the ups and downs and the requirements of its new environment. Yes, we will win and you will lose. For you are not able to rid your minds of the obsolete Taylorisms that we never had.*

Dr. Elbie paused as he came to the end. He looked at the class and asked, "Any comments?" The room was hushed. No one said anything. Dr. Elbie went on, "When you come right down to it, Matsushita is right, but Taylorism is only one of the reasons. Were any of you bothered by this quote?"

Jim was very uncomfortable while Dr. Elbie was reading the quotation and without raising his hand said, "I think that he is probably right but he has misjudged Americans. I think that we are up to the challenge that he gave us. I know we can make this place better. That is all I can control. I am looking forward to any change that can turn this place around."

Dr. Elbie smiled as he continued. "Thank you, Jim. Does anyone else have anything to say? Is he right? Does anyone ever listen to your ideas? What happens when you have a good idea?" Dr. Elbie waited for an answer and no one said anything. No one was going to touch any of those questions.

* Manufacturing Engineering, February 1988, p. 15

So he continued, "And Mr. Matsushita was right. I talk, you listen. I have ideas, you don't. Is that the way it is? Do you really believe this?"

Everyone was just sitting like a bunch of dummies, and no one was saying anything. Dr. Elbie continued, "So no one wants to admit that Mr. Matsushita was right or wrong? Does anybody hear me? Help, I'm sinking!" Everyone smiled at his bad attempts to get us talking, but still no one was talking.

Dr. Elbie kept right on, "Is Mr. Matsushita talking about this company and no one wants to say so? OK, let's try this. Mr. Grimes knows that his company isn't working quite right. How does he know that?"

Roland Diamond, the Vice President of Sales, raised his hand and Dr. Elbie acknowledged him with a quick nod. Roland said, "Jack, I'll bail you out of this stalemate. I would assume that Mr. Grimes knows because he isn't making any money. We are here to make money and we aren't making enough. He has to change something."

Dr. Elbie went on, "Right, Roland. You are very right. The goal of this or any other business is to make money. And when it doesn't, something has to be fixed. My colleagues and I are here to help you fix it. The process involves change and very few people like to change. However, I love to change things and I won't be satisfied here until change is accepted. The Japanese have a term for this. It's called *kaisen*, and it means 'continuous improvement.' Americans have a difficult time with that, and say things like, If it ain't broke, don't fix it.

"Personally, I'm always going to try to change things around to make them better. This training process will give you tremendous insight into what your priorities of change should be. You should never change just to change. You should only change something that you can make better.

"During this training you're going to make your company better. You're going to make it profitable and you'll be very proud of your results, but you can never rest. My third grade teacher, Miss Foley, had a saying. Here Dr. Elbie put a transparency on the overhead projector and read:

> Good, Better, Best
> Never let it rest
> 'Til the Good is Better and
> The Better is Best
> —Miss Foley School of Management

The New Turnaround

"I really believe in what she said. That is why I call that quote the basis of the Miss Foley School of Management. It says it all. Everyone in America had a Miss Foley. She was the teacher who really knew what was going on and touched our lives. Did everyone here have someone like her?"

As Dr. Elbie looked around the room everyone nodded positively that they had had a similar teacher. Dr. Elbie went on, "And I'm not going to rest until this place is *THE BEST."*

Buck jumped up and yelled, "Right on, my man. That's our goal, let's make this place the best pump manufacturer in the world. That should be our goal."

Mr. Grimes asked to speak and he began, "I agree, and I think we should be well on our way by the time the training is over. Buck, as I understand it, during the training you'll confront a lot of your own ideas about work, about production and about responsibility. By the time this training is over, *you and your co-workers will be responsible for your own work.* Not your foreman, not the plant superintendent, not Dr. Elbie, *YOU.* And when you do that Quality Pump will be the best.

"We need to fix this company. We need to improve it. We need to change. I know that this change is not going to be very comfortable for some of you. Change never is! So as we move forward, feel free to give me a call. Or, since I'm going to be spending more time on the shop floor now, stop me if you have any problems that you want to discuss."

Mr. Grimes handed the class back to Dr. Elbie. Dr. Elbie continued, "I'm gonna give you people something that students in a Harvard MBA class spend tens-of-thousands of dollars to learn. By the time this training is over you'll be able to apply this process even better than they will. We are going to make Quality Pump profitable and you people are going to lead the charge.

While he was talking he had wandered around the room a little bit, now he returned to the blackboard and wrote:

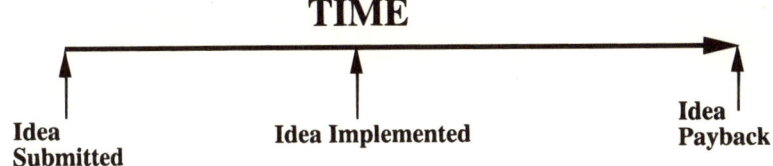

"This is what this training is all about," Dr. Elbie said. "Pay attention because this is really all you need to know to understand what we're going to do in this class. We're going to examine the process and the time it takes to go from the input of an idea into your system until the money flows into the company. The shorter the time, the more money you make.

Then Dr. Elbie wrote:

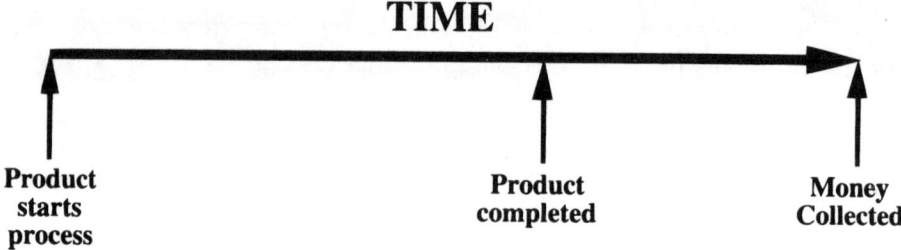

He explained, "There are many things that happen to produce a product but the most important is to start with an order, produce it, deliver it and then collect money for the product. Everyone in the organization should be geared to understanding this cycle. The order is not complete until the money is collected. So everyone should be focused on insuring that that happens. You'll notice that I said the word *you*, not the company. I say that because if you come up with an idea that saves the company time, everyone benefits. You will all see it in your paycheck because John's agreed that if you help him improve the company's position, you will see it in raises and bonuses."

At that moment all eyes in the classroom turned to Mr. Grimes, who nodded in agreement.

As the next illustration shows it also applies to new product development.

Idea-Time to Market
(Profit vs. Time)

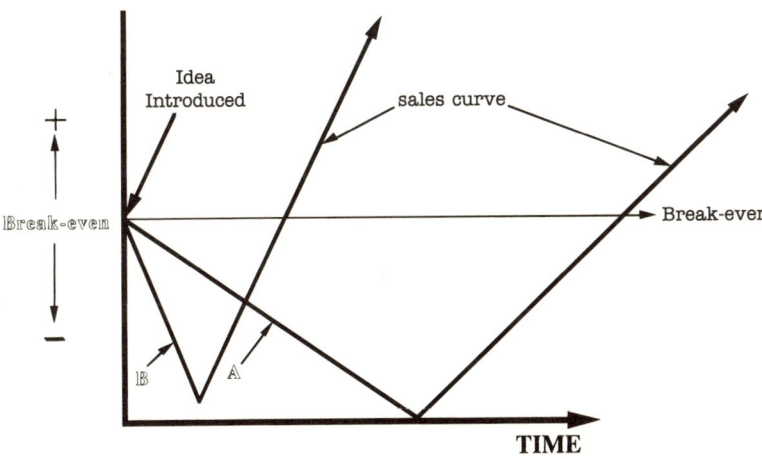

"In this example, the idea is generated at some initial point and money is allocated to the project. As the money is spent, it follows the curve designated A. This is of course a simple graph but it makes the point. If you can get the idea to market quicker, line B, you have actually spent less money because you do not have the interest investment required to support the longer development time, line B. But more importantly, you may create more market enthusiasm and end up with a selling curve with a greater slope as noted. In other words, the faster you implement an idea, the quicker the market will see its effect. This applies to products as well as process improvements."

Dr. Elbie continued, "You people are a major asset to this company, even more important than the buildings and machinery. By the way, Mr. Grimes, I am impressed by the new twenty-six-axis robot that you have in the back."

Mr. Grimes was surprised. He didn't follow Dr. Elbie's comment. He didn't own any robot. What was Dr. Elbie talking about? "Jack, I don't follow you. I don't own a twenty-six-axis robot."

Dr. Elbie smiled, "John, most of you never think of people in this way, but a human being has two arms and two legs. Each arm and each leg can move in six different degrees of freedom: forward, back, sideways, and in three rotational degrees of freedom. The head can move up and down and turn sideways for two more degrees of freedom." He looked at Mr. Grimes and said, "Now do you see what I mean?"

Mr. Grimes smiled and responded, "You got me. That's a good point."

Dr. Elbie went on, "How do you think that any company would treat a computer that could reason, could be taught to speak a foreign language and could program other computers? They would certainly treat it with great care.

"I know that some of you are thinking 'Great, here comes some other jerk with that feel good about yourself crap.' Well, you have every right to think that, but it's up to me to change your mind and I am confident that my associates and I can do just that. There's one important factor that you have to consider. Mr. Grimes is putting his money behind my mouth." That got a small chuckle from us. You could see Mr. Grimes shift in his chair. I think he was a little surprised by what Dr. Elbie said.

Dr. Elbie went on, "Let me tell you a little story that might help explain how I got into this business. I started out selling high technology solutions to manufacturers all over the United States. They would hire the company that I worked for to solve a problem that their own people couldn't solve. It was usually a pretty tough problem. I liked that because I got to look at just about every manufacturing process you can imagine."

Dr. Elbie looked off in the direction of Buck, in the back of the room. Then he turned to the class, smiled, and asked, "Have any of you ever wondered how you make toilet paper?"

Everyone laughed.

Dr. Elbie continued, "No, I really mean it. Do any of you ever think about all the things that you use in your daily life that are made by people just like you. Let me take something else. Do any of you know how paper is made? Do you know how steel is rolled into flat sheets? Do you know how money is made? Where they print it?"

At this point, Buck got into it, "You know what this sounds like. I once watched a kids' show and the host got into these kinds of questions with the kids. He started asking a bunch of little kids really weird questions, just like the ones you're asking. Only his were even weirder. He was asking kids questions like, 'How do you get toothpaste into the tubes? How do you get fuzz on tennis balls?' Man, were those questions strange. And you know what, he got me thinking.

"This question has been bugging me for a long time. Maybe you have seen something on this. How do you mass produce castings, like parts for my Harley? I know how castings are made. That's not what I mean. I am not familiar with the way castings are mass produced. How do they do mass production of something like a casting?"

Dr. Elbie looked at Buck and asked him his name. He responded, and Dr. Elbie continued. "That's a good question. I've been in several casting plants. I have a few films on various casting plants that you might like to see. I think that I have one on a plant that I toured in China and several on different casting plants in the United States. One of the plants is about two miles from here.

"Anyway, I am glad you asked me that question. I could answer it but I have another idea. Buck, can we talk after class? I think I'd like to give you a fun homework assignment. However, I want to talk with Mr. Grimes first."

Buck joked, "Are you going to send me to China?"

"No," Dr. Elbie responded, "nothing that exciting!" Then he continued, "There are some real neat things that the host was trying to do with that TV show. I also remember watching it with my kids. I really liked it.

"I have an idea about what he was doing. I think that he was trying to test the children's imaginations. That's exactly what we want to do in this training. We want to test your imaginations, not your knowledge. There is a company in Wisconsin that takes great pride in getting the workers involved in all aspects of running the business. Ralph Stayer, the owner of the Johnsonville Sausage Company, believes very strongly and says, 'Companies don't care what you know, they care what you do!'

"And that's my position as well. We're going to make you do. We're going to go where no man has gone before. We're going to look and see if there are any better ways to do things than the ways you do them now. I believe that all of you have some good ideas and what we need to do is create a system that will allow them to get implemented in a timely fashion.

"Let me give you an example of what I am talking about. In one of the projects that I was working on we were having a difficult time getting the equipment to work. After a week of trying to install the new equipment the plant manager was getting edgy and I was beginning to get worried that the new equipment was not going to work. As his anxiety level rose, so did the anxiety of all the people who were working on the project. The mechanical, electrical and the industrial engineering departments could not even identify the problem.

"After struggling with the equipment for several days, I was standing off to one side of the machine trying to figure out how I was going to make this damn thing work. One of the workers on the production line, her name was Mabel, came over to me. She asked me what was going on, so I told her. I explained the problem to her.

"In about fifteen seconds she made an observation that none of the engineers had made. Her idea actually identified and solved the problem no one else could. We implemented her solution and the equipment worked perfectly.

"Why is this story significant? If we had asked her earlier, she could've participated in the design process and she might have saved us all that lost time. None of us thought of asking for any help from the line workers. After all, what would they know that all those engineers didn't?

"There's another angle to this story. Mabel was offering her help and I listened to her. I could have taken all the credit for the idea, as managers had done with me before. When all the engineers complimented me on the good idea, I hesitated for a moment, then I pointed Mabel out and told them it was her idea. The senior member of the team went over and thanked her. Not only was she grateful, it was probably the first time any manager in the plant had ever thanked her for anything. That taught me that managers and supervisors aren't the only source of good ideas in a company.

"I want to emphasize that there are no dumb ideas. As Thomas Edison said, we may have one hundred ideas and only one good one. The other ninety-nine are not bad ideas, they're merely ninety-nine ways not to solve the problem.

"In this class, we're going to solve problems. We're going to identify the problems, figure out how to determine their financial effect on the company, and learn lots of ways to solve them using *your ideas*. Not mine.

"My role here is simply to serve as the facilitator. I'll lead you in a discovery process which will use some new tools, but the bulk of the ideas in these classes will come from your own discussions. It is called discovery because we are going to discover a whole new way of looking at your job. You'll also soon discover that you can contribute to the improvement of the company. We're going to listen to your ideas and

The New Turnaround

if they make sense we will implement them. If the idea can save the company a lot of money, we'll put it at the top of our priority list.

"After a couple of weeks, we'll set up the Productivity Review Board. The PRB will meet weekly to review your ideas.

"During the training we will agree on a format for an Idea Committee. It'll review all ideas for productivity improvement or waste elimination. Any questions?"

Tony was fidgeting. I figured that he was upset from being in the classroom and not in the shop.

Dr. Elbie continued, "Our training program over the next several weeks will look at wastes in the company operations. We're going to identify wastes in the business and then we're going to figure out ways to eliminate them. There's nothing that we're going to do that is beyond any of your capabilities. Either I or one of my associates will facilitate the process of identifying the waste and establishing cost-effective solutions to eliminate the waste. We may offer suggestions that you might not otherwise consider. In all cases, *you* will be making all the decisions about how to solve the problems that you have identified.

"The VAP program simply provides a framework to discuss the solutions. We'll teach you ways to look at problems and discuss solutions that everyone in this room can easily understand. VAP is merely a system that we've put together using a number of techniques, some of my own and some borrowed from other productivity consultants. The Japanese, Henry Ford, Tom Peters, Edwards Deming, and a lot of other people have all had good ideas on how to improve production."

Tony apparently couldn't hold it in any longer and yelled out, "This is crap. This just another one of those motivational programs. All you're really here for is the money. Personally, I think this class is a crock of shit and you can quote me on that."

Everyone in the class turned to look at Tony. Mr. Grimes started to respond but Dr. Elbie interrupted him, "Pardon me, Mr. Grimes," he said, "I started this discussion." Everyone was looking at Dr. Elbie. The tension in the room was pretty thick.

As Dr. Elbie faced Tony, you could see that he wasn't bothered by him at all. It almost seemed like he had been anticipating it. He paused in front of Tony, turned and walked to the board at the front of the room and wrote:

No Blame!

"Who can tell me what this means?" No one raised a hand, so Dr. Elbie continued. "No Blame means exactly what it says. In the context of this business and in American business in general it means moving away from the notion of blaming someone else for your problems at work. Traditionally, management has blamed the workers and the workers have blamed management for a whole range of issues.

"As Mr. Grimes and Mr. Daley will tell you, negotiations of union contracts are often carried out under a cloud of animosity and distrust. Labor and management spend more time and energy trying to outfox each other than they do trying to understand how they can help each other be more productive."

Then he looked in the direction of Mr. Grimes and Mr. Daley. "They always blame the other side. Unfortunately, when you blame someone else, you take away any possibility of coming up with the real solution to the problem. This extends all the way down to the shop floor. For example, a foreman might blame a machine operator saying, 'Jack screwed up that part.' So obviously, he doesn't look any further. He's found somebody to blame.

"The reason Jack screwed up the part is *not* that he's incompetent. It's that the bearing on the lathe that he's complained about for the last three years is worn and the material won't spin true. When we stop blaming Jack we can begin to look for the real cause of the problem; we can come up with real solutions to real problems."

He turned to Tony and asked him his name. Dr. Elbie then said, "Tony, thank you for opening up the discussion. You may have a good point there. Does anyone else feel the same as Tony?" A few hands went up.

"First of all," Dr. Elbie said, "I've got to admit that I don't agree with you. I really think that this training process *can* turn this plant around. I could stand here all day long and tell you all the good things I'm going to do for you, but would you believe me?"

He stared at Tony and waited for an answer. Tony shook his head no.

"At least we can start by agreeing on that point because I don't expect you to believe anything I say. Judge me only by what you and your co-workers accomplish during the training and the months following it. That's all I ask of you. Is that fair?"

Tony nodded in agreement.

At that moment Dr. Elbie grabbed everyone's attention again when he asked, "What is the purpose of this business?" He looked right at Tony as if he expected him to answer.

One of the other guys, named Steve, jumped in: "To make money," he said with a sly grin.

Dr. Elbie then looked at Mr. Grimes and asked him if he agreed. Mr. Grimes didn't look very pleased to be dragged into this conversation.

"Of course," he said, "we want to make money. That is the objective of this business, isn't it? That's the objective of any business."

Dr. Elbie clapped his hands once and laughed, "OK, we've got labor and management agreeing already! So the question is what do we do to make money? What is the customer willing to pay for?"

The class seemed to get a little restless when Dr. Elbie posed these questions. People were shifting around in their chairs and looking at each other and at Dr. Elbie. It seemed like these questions opened a whole new can of worms.

Dr. Elbie went back to the blackboard and in big letters he wrote the word VALUE. "Value, that's what the customer is willing to pay for," he said. "The customer is not willing to pay for the controller's salary, although the controller is necessary. He's not willing to pay for the inefficiencies in your shipping department. He's only willing to pay for the added value of the product. The real question we have to ask is, what adds value to a product?"

Buck was irritated that Dr. Elbie had made a negative comment about his department. He jumped up and snapped, "Look, Elbie, we do good work in the shipping department." All six-feet-six-inches of Buck was now standing. He went on, "I don't like being picked on. My people do a good job. We do the best we can. We aren't perfect, but who is? I'd like to see anyone else run the shipping dock any better!" And he sat himself down.

Dr. Elbie smiled tentatively. He wasn't intimidated by Buck, "Why is there a problem, Buck?"

"Because we get bad information about shipments, we get wrong materials packed in boxes, we get all the screwups of the rest of the company thrown in our laps. We can do good work, but we need help from the other departments we service. We can't do it alone. As long as we do, we're going to look bad. It's always our fault." Buck was pretty angry.

Dr. Elbie looked directly at Buck and asked him, "Would you mind letting me table this discussion for a few days? I'll get back to addressing it, but let me have a few days before we get to your problem. I think some other things may come up and your problem will look a little different."

Buck nodded glumly and said, "I'll wait, but don't pick on my department any more. You got that?"

Dr. Elbie laughed. "Yes, Buck, I got that. And I promise to leave your department alone for the next two days.

"So let's get back to the issue we were discussing earlier. What adds value? Does boring a required hole in a valve body add value? Does setting up the machine to drill the hole add value? Does delivering the product to the customer add value? I need some answers. What do you say?"

Slowly, a hand or two went up. Billy, my lead man, didn't raise his hand, he just said, "Doing the setup and boring the hole add value, making a delivery doesn't."

Dr. Elbie smiled and said, "Are you sure about that?"

Billy was a little uncertain, but he said, "If you don't do the setup you can't drill the hole; if you don't drill the hole the valve won't work." By this time Billy seemed to be getting a little defiant. "And you know, Dr. Elbie, if the valve don't work, nobody's gonna buy it. And I say deliveries don't add value."

Buck was angry and stood up, "Look, asshole," and he pointed at Billy, "don't pick on my department."

Dr. Elbie interrupted, "Buck, we aren't picking on your department. Billy was just making an observation.

"Let's think about what Billy just said. If the customer only wants to pay for a working valve he isn't concerned with setup. He's only concerned that the hole is there, that the parts are machined to the tolerances that are specified, that the valve functions, and it's affordable and dependable.

"So we can say that value is added only when the parts are actually being machined or assembled.* The customer is only interested in paying for a machined part. We can place every function, in this or any other business, into two categories: those that add value and those that don't. When you are doing a setup are you adding value?"

The blueprint shop manager was a little tentative, but he raised his

---

* Value-Added—There is a good deal of discussion in the literature about the meaning of *value-added*. I could probably get few economists to agree with my definition.

hand and said, "I'm kind of confused, Dr. Elbie. What's the difference between a value-added job and a non-value added job? I run the blueprint shop and I'd hate to think that I was being paid for not adding value. You're implying I don't add value, but I think that my job is necessary. Do I add value or not?"

Dr. Elbie looked at the class and asked, "Does anyone have any help for this gentleman here? Does the blueprint shop manager add value to this business? What do you think?"

Jim was sitting at the back of the room and raised his hand. Dr. Elbie looked at him and said, "Go ahead, Jim. What do you have to say?"

"I thought for a minute that I didn't have an answer, but it suddenly hit me. Phil's job in the blueprint shop doesn't add any value, but it *is* necessary."

Dr. Elbie agreed, "Correct. In essence, he is necessary waste. He doesn't add value, but we can't do our jobs without his services. Buck also falls into that category. Buck is necessary waste or essential support. Not every job in this plant is support; some are just plain waste. When you load or unload a milling machine, you're not adding value to the product. You're just wasting time."

While he was talking he drew the following on the board:

Three Functions Present

In Every Business

Jim asked, "So, you're implying that setup is a waste. Right?"

Dr. Elbie replied, "I don't know. I asked the question first. Does anyone else have an idea about this?"

Tony and Gus had their hands up instantly. I could see that after Dr. Elbie's statement they were both real hot. Dr. Elbie called on Gus, while Tony fumed. Gus stood up, redfaced, and said, "You mean to tell me that me and my people don't add value here? If it wasn't for us, this place would close down in a damn minute!"

Dr. Elbie replied, "Gus, I'm not saying that your work isn't valuable to this company. I am saying that the work that you do does not fall into the *value added* category. It falls into the category of waste or essential support. And by the way, I'm sure the company could learn to stumble along without you." Gus got even redder in the face, but quietly sat down.

"OK, let's get it out in the open," Dr. Elbie said. "The truth is everybody here is *expendable* and that includes Mr. Grimes." Mr. Grimes got a surprised look on his face but said nothing.

Dr. Elbie continued, "There's going to be a test at the end of this training. It's going to be pass or fail. If you pass, the company stays in business; if you fail, this plant will end up like Osgood's. If that happens, you will all be expendable, including Mr. Grimes."

Dr. Elbie sure had succeeded in getting our attention. You could feel it all of a sudden because everyone got serious.

Buck was a biker and he ran the loading dock with an iron hand. He also drove one of the delivery trucks. He was a big guy and had long black hair and a scraggly beard that was starting to turn gray in spots. Buck had been a good friend of Jack's when Jack was the plant superintendent. Everybody knew that he wasn't exactly thrilled when Jack got fired. He had made it very clear to anyone who would listen that he did not like Jim because Jim had replaced his buddy. He also seemed to dislike the changes that Jim had been making in the plant.

Buck stood up and said, "Look, Dr. Elbie, if I don't deliver the pumps to our customers, we won't have any customers. They'll buy from somebody who will deliver. I know for damn sure I'm not wasting my time making deliveries."

I could tell by the way he said it that he was angry. He had figured out quickly that his job didn't add value and he didn't like Billy pointing it out in front of the whole class.

Dr. Elbie looked right at Buck and didn't seem at all intimidated by his stare. He went on, "You're right, Buck, they will buy from someone

The New Turnaround

who delivers. You've got to understand, a job that adds value is not superior to one that is essential support. We just need to separate the two so that we can get a clear picture of what really goes on in this business.

"We want to maximize added value, minimize support and eliminate waste. Some of you are probably thinking, If they minimize support, there goes my job. That couldn't be further from the truth. The market is there for Quality Pump to expand and to sell more product. What we have to do is get the efficiency of this plant to satisfy the new demand."

Dr. Elbie asked Buck if he was feeling nervous about his job. Buck replied that he was. He told Dr. Elbie that he had a wife and three kids and couldn't afford to be laid off.

Dr. Elbie said, "Would you have more confidence in your job if you were delivering one hundred fifty pumps a day instead of sixty?" Buck replied that he would.

Tony raised his hand and asked, "Just how do you propose to do that? We're already scrambling to get the orders out that we got now."

Dr. Elbie went to the board and wrote the word WASTE. He turned around, pointed to it and said, "By eliminating waste, that's how. Much of what you do in the shop, and for that matter, in the whole company, can be done more efficiently and with less waste. Can somebody give me an example of waste?" Hands shot up all over the place.

Dr. Elbie called on a person who worked in the assembly department and she said, "A lot of times an order will be returned because the inlet or outlet pipe on the pump is the wrong size. The engineering department is always giving us the wrong specs. We get tired of having to do the work over."

Then a guy from engineering jumped up and said, "Hey, we can only give the specs that we get from the sales department. We've talked to them before about giving us the wrong information, but it doesn't seem to do any good."

The whole class turned around to look at Roland and Bonnie. Roland was vice president of sales and Bonnie was one of his people. She sold over the phone and was supposed to be good at it. All I knew about her was that she was pretty standoffish. When she did come out to the shop, she acted like the machines and the workers were going to attack her.

Everyone in the class was looking right at them. Roland just looked icily back at the class, and Bonnie looked upset. She tried to tell us that we didn't understand the pressure that she was under to make her sales goals. She insisted that it was only natural that mistakes were sometimes made.

The guy from engineering said that it was more than occasionally and everyone in the class agreed.

Dr. Elbie shouted, "Hey, wait a minute! Everybody cool it!" We all turned back to him. He was standing at the board, pointing to the *No Blame* that he had written. "No blame!" he shouted. "Don't blame Roland and Bonnie. That isn't going to solve the problem. Bonnie may make mistakes on some of the orders, but she's not the only salesperson. She may be part of the problem, but she's not the whole problem.

"Instead of finding people to blame, let's see if we can make some sense out of this problem now that we've identified it. Let's try to quantify the size of the problem. Let's see if we can see the extent of the problem in the business and how it creates waste."

Dr. Elbie was really excited. I could tell that he saw something interesting about this problem. He looked at everyone and asked, "Shall we try to solve this problem?"

Everyone agreed that we should. Dr. Elbie began, "In order to get a handle on this problem, on the size of the waste, we need to do a little calculation. We need to do this calculation in order to prioritize the problems, to see which ones need immediate attention. Let's see what we discover."

Dr. Elbie wrote $25 per hour on the blackboard. "To begin, we need to find a way to quantify the size of this waste. We have to relate the wasted time in processing the order to the inaccurate data on the sales order. We'll use the $25 per hour figure because it represents the cost to Mr. Grimes, or the company, of keeping the average person employed at this company. In other words, it represents the cost to open the doors and run the business. Is this a reasonable number?"

The engineers both raised their hands. Dr. Elbie acknowledged the older of the two who responded, "It seems to me that it must cost a lot more to employ somebody than $25 an hour. My God, if you consider benefits, the cost of the building, insurance and all that, it must cost a lot more."

Dr. Elbie looked over at Mr. Grimes and asked, "Would you care to comment?"

Mr. Grimes smiled and said, "Of course, it costs a lot more than $25 an hour to keep an employee on the payroll. A lot more. But as you told me the other day, if we use $25 an hour, our results for the sizing of wastes will be conservative, on the low side. No one will argue with our results. If they are bad at $25 an hour, then they will be terrible when the real number is used."

Dr. Elbie continued right where Mr. Grimes ended. "And we really don't need to be rocket scientists to do these calculations. We'll use $25 per hour in quantifying all wastes that we identify. The real figure is probably a lot higher, but we'd all scare ourselves if we were dealing in real numbers.

"For starters, Jim, could you get me some figures for assembly rework over the last couple of months? We should really only focus on rework that has been attributed to errors on the sales order. If you get the complete list of rework problems, then we can make some decisions about the extent of any errors resulting from incorrect sales orders."

Jim and Patty, the assembly lead person, left the room. While they were gone Dr. Elbie made two columns on the board. The first column was entitled WASTE, the second SIZE.

Pretty soon Jim and Patty came back. Each of them was holding a bunch of papers. Patty sat down at one of the tables. Jim joined her and together they went over the paperwork.

When they were finished, they had seven or eight pieces of paper. Jim took the papers over and handed them to Dr. Elbie.

Dr. Elbie glanced at a couple of them as he walked over to the projector in the back of the room. "Would someone please pull the screen back down?" Dr. Elbie asked.

He placed the first sheet on the projector and we looked at the screen.

PRODUCTION ORDER

CUSTOMER: Nova Industrial Plumbing and Pump	WORK ORDER NO.: L-06335
SALESMAN: Carl Race	
APPROVED: R. Diamond	

QUANTITY	DESCRIPTION
80	No. 255, pump w/ 1 3/4" inlet pipe
30	No. 155, pump w/ 1 3/4" inlet pipe

255's need 2½" inlet

DUE DATE: ASAP

Scrawled across the work order in red felt pen were the words: 255s need 2½" inlet.

Dr. Elbie looked at the screen and said, "You can see that Bonnie's not the problem on this one!" Everyone laughed as Bonnie clasped her hands and looked toward the ceiling in mock prayer.

He went on, "Now, let's quantify the rework on this one order. Jim, can you tell me how much time and materials were needed to make this order right?"

Jim said, "I think Patty would have a better handle on what it took than me."

Patty said, "The 255 can use several inlet valves. The 1¾" and the 2½" use the same valve body; only the inlet size on the top casting is different."

Dr. Elbie asked, "So, did you change inlet valves?"

"No," Patty replied, "we didn't have enough of the 2½" valves made up. Besides that, it takes a long time to disconnect all the plumbing and wiring between the valve and the pump. We decided just to change the top part of the valve body and replace it with the 2½" inlet."

Dr. Elbie asked her how long it took. Patty said, "Each valve body only took about five minutes to replace, but we had a problem on many of them because the sealant we use on the diaphragm would not break clean as we disassembled the valves. As a result, the diaphragm would tear. We tried to go in first and cut the sealant with razor knives, but quite often we ended up cutting the diaphragm too. And if the diaphragm got cut, we couldn't use it again."

Everyone was paying a lot of attention to Patty as she continued, "Many of these pumps had been sitting in inventory for a long time. They were causing the most problems. Trying to separate the valve body without tearing the diaphragm took about fifteen to twenty minutes. So the whole job, including re-boxing, averaged about twenty to twenty-five minutes for each pump. About three quarters of the valves needed to be cut to get them apart, and we probably lost about twenty percent of those.

"We didn't have enough diaphragms to replace the ones we tore and our supplier in town didn't have enough either. I had to send one of the apprentices into the city to pick some up. That took about three hours.

"I know it doesn't sound economical to try and save the diaphragm, since they only cost about eighty cents each, but we weren't sure we could get replacements and everyone was on our ass to get the pumps out."

Dr. Elbie said, "Patty, while you were talking, I did a little quick math. Your people spent about thirty hours in fixing the pumps. You also lost three hours when the driver went into town to get the parts you needed. That's a total of thirty-three hours. At $25 an hour that comes to $825. That's a substantial amount of money. That's more than any profit potential generated by that order.

"OK now, this is just one isolated incident of rework. Think about all the rework that goes on in this plant. From the shop floor to the corporate offices, even a misdirected delivery would amount to a substantial amount of money. WASTE!"

He stopped and repeated the word, "Waste! You see that? You lost $825 on just one order. That's waste and that, my friends, is what's killing American business. Politicians, union leaders, owners and CEOs of huge corporations say that we need protection in the form of tariffs or other government incentives to survive against our overseas competitors, but it just isn't true. *We only need protection from ourselves!* I'm sorry to be up on my soapbox, but this is serious business! Just think: *How competitive would America be, if all the wastes in our organizations were eliminated? Would we need government protection?"*

And then Dr. Elbie stopped. He asked in a very calm voice, "Does this upset any of you?"

Everyone nodded yes, and I felt a strong buzz of excitement in the room. He really had us going.

As Dr. Elbie continued on through the rest of the work orders, the class did the quantification calculations. We were all stunned. In just seven incidents of rework, we found over $11,000 worth of waste. And that was only during a two-month period in one area of the company! Mr. Grimes looked disgusted, but he certainly was paying attention!

Dr. Elbie said, "I don't often assign homework with these classes, but today I'm going to do just that. I want you all to think about this first problem we encountered and see if you can come up with any solutions. Remember, the simpler, the better." The class was over for the day. I felt kind of nervous as I left the room, but also excited.

6

The next morning the classroom was abuzz with people and groups comparing their solutions. All of our solutions seemed pretty much the same. I was amazed that we could have such a big problem for so long without anyone noticing. I guess that as the company got bigger, problems like this just became the accepted way of doing business.

When Dr. Elbie entered the room, we quieted down. He looked over at the chair where Mr. Grimes had sat yesterday. The chair was empty.

Dr. Elbie was visibly annoyed, but then he smiled and said, "Well, how'd we do last night?" Gus was practically climbing out of his chair, so Dr. Elbie called on him.

Gus said, "First of all, I want to say that this solution was a group effort. All of you know Frank Brooks. Well, he was the one who came up with the original idea. The whole setup crew and Tony's crew worked on refining it." Frank and Tony seemed to really appreciate the recognition.

Gus continued, "What we did was use one of the work sheets that we use to list the tools and jigs for setup as a model. We listed most of the pumps, valves and control units that are required to build about 70% of our business. It turns out that about 24% of our parts account for 72% of our business!"

I couldn't figure Gus out. First, he acts like a jerk, and now suddenly he was really into this program. He stood up in front of everyone with great pride as he led the discussion.

Gus continued, "Anyway, we've listed all the pump numbers on the left of this sheet and listed all the possible valve and control numbers to the right. The only thing that the person taking the order has to do is check the appropriate boxes. We've left some space at the bottom of the order form to write in any custom jobs. Does anyone have any questions?" No one raised a hand. They just clapped as he sat down. It was clear that Gus's solution was simple and workable.

Bonnie raised her hand and said, "That's an excellent start. We're using an order form where we have to write the order out in longhand. This idea will make things a lot better.

"I still think we have a problem after the order gets into the sales department and makes its way to the shop floor. I went back over my sales contracts and found that I had made a couple of errors. I also found that there were a few transcription errors from my paperwork to the shop floor. There're too many opportunities to make a mistake every time an order is transcribed from one form to another."

Bernard said, "In the engineering department, as part of the CAD/CAM system, there is a barcode scanner. If we could standardize the forms, I could write a program that would recognize the boxes and download the information on the order right into the computer. We could eliminate a lot of steps and mistakes as well."

The class began to applaud again because most of us found Bernard very difficult. He was from France and felt that most Americans were beneath him. For some reason, he was cooperating.

Dr. Elbie was forced to raise his hands and ask for silence. He said, "Great! That's an excellent beginning, but we still have a long way to go."

Before he could continue, the door opened and Mr. Grimes entered. He asked Dr. Elbie if he could address the class. "First of all, I must apologize to you and to Dr. Elbie for being late this morning. I had a meeting that could not be cancelled. To avoid that in the future, I have rearranged my schedule so that I can be in this class throughout the rest of the training sessions.

"After what we discovered in class yesterday and talking again with Jack Prescott last night, I really see the value of this training. Originally, when Dr. Elbie told me the value that I would get from the training, I figured he was just overoptimistic. Yesterday though, I saw why he feels so strongly about where this training will lead.

"I'm really excited. This is going to be fun. I can see how we're going to follow this process. And it's important not only for you, but also for the company and me as well."

After Mr. Grimes took his seat, Dr. Elbie went to the board and started writing. He said, "Thank you very much, Mr. Grimes.

"OK, like I said, we've made an excellent beginning. There are a few more things we must do with wastes. The first thing I want you to do is to take a couple of minutes and list all the wastes that you can think of. Remember, *NO BLAME*. And be honest with your appraisal of a problem."

When we finished, Dr. Elbie listed all the wastes that we had given him one by one on the board. Many of us had listed the same wastes, so he put the number of times each waste was listed next to it. In all, we had identified thirty-seven wastes.

Dr. Elbie went to the overhead projector and put a transparency on the machine. He turned to the class: "Before we get into any more specific wastes, let's look at waste from another perspective. In this chart, I have shown a representation of what we call our Gap Analysis."

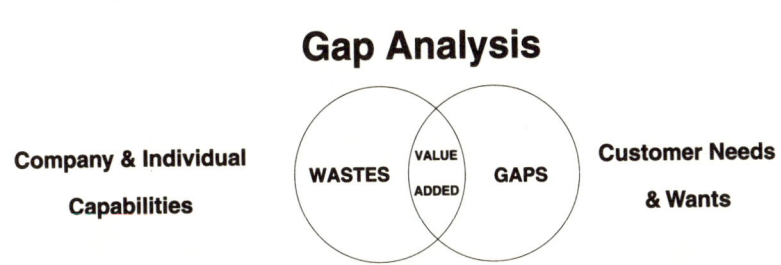

A gap on this chart is the difference between what you can deliver and what the customer wants. Remember this whole business is based on providing products to customers. The customers have a number of wants. You are able to deliver some of those, which is the area of overlap that is shown as the value-added section of the chart. Now that is what you are trying to deliver—value-added products to your customers. As we get into this process, the goal will be to examine what you are doing here, what your capabilities are and whether any customers want what you have."

Roland jumped in, "You mean to tell me that we will be looking at the capabilities of this company compared to our competition. Very interesting, Dr. Elbie. Bonnie and I just spent about two months collecting some of that information."

Dr. Elbie smiled while responding to Roland, "And we will have a chance to see how we stack up against your competition. How does it look?"

Roland continued, "I think we are OK, but we are missing some market opportunities because of some holes in our product offering. Maybe we can look at that later. We certainly need to look at a number of new product introductions."

"Before I get off this subject," Dr. Elbie continued, "can I have a show of hands? How many of you know who your competition is and what products they offer?" A few hands went up. "Roland, would you be prepared to share that information with us next week?"

"Absolutely, I guess I see where we need more education for everybody in the company. I just assumed that everyone knew our competition. I do. But I guess all the rest of you aren't exposed to our competition to the same extent that I am. I would love to share this information with all the classes. I'll make room for that on my schedule next week and spend twenty to thirty minutes in each class next week. Is that OK, Mr. Grimes?"

Mr. Grimes nodded a firm yes and stood up, "Jack, will we be able to do everything that needs to be done to fix my business? Every time we talk, another major hurdle comes up. When will this stop?"

Dr. Elbie walked over to Mr. Grimes and said, "Probably never. But, does everyone in this room feel that we're making progress?" Everyone gave a vocal yes. Dr. Elbie continued, "Mr. Grimes, this process is made up of a large number of little steps. It's the way we eat an elephant, a bite at a time. We'll make it, just be patient." Mr. Grimes sat down and let out a big sigh.

Dr. Elbie went back to the transparency and pointed to the waste area, "And this is waste created by you when you have capabilities that no one wants. It would be like having an expert welder when you didn't need that capability. It's a nice capability but it would be a waste if it was a skill that you didn't need. That is what is meant by this chart. Waste appears not just as inefficiencies but in wasted talent and failing to deliver the wants of the customer. Does everybody understand?"

Everybody indicated they understood, so Dr. Elbie went on, "During the rest of this week we'll spend our time identifying and categorizing wastes. You've been pretty good so far, but I just bet there are more wastes lurking out there in the business. We've opened your eyes a little. Let's question everything and see if you can find some more wastes."

He paused as Tony raised his hand and asked, "If we know where the problems are, why do we need to put them in categories other than size?" For all his bad-mouthing of the training, Tony was also getting into it.

Dr. Elbie replied, "That's a good question. The reason we do this is to see who and what is affected by the changes we propose. For instance, we will talk about the twelve categories of waste. As we identify wastes, we'll begin to associate a waste with a category. We try to group wastes into categories because if we have ten separate wastes dealing with a specific waste category, maybe we can see a bigger problem that needs to be solved.

"One reason that we group the wastes together is to help get rid of them. We don't have any other reason. It just makes the solution easier to grasp. If we group wastes of like type, then we can get a handle on how certain parts of the system are working together. By grouping like wastes, many times we are able to see problems that don't crop up otherwise. For example, when we put all the wastes of waiting together, we see lots of problems because the system doesn't keep material and information flowing smoothly. By identifying the wastes and grouping like wastes, we get a clearer picture of the problems.

"Another reason for grouping the wastes is that some analysis techniques work better on some wastes, some on others. You'll see what I mean by this later," Dr. Elbie said.

"As we continue to move forward, we will implement solutions to one problem and find that another problem shows up to take its place. In fact, I can say emphatically: *Today's solution is tomorrow's problem!*

"For example," he said, "let's take the waste that we discussed earlier, the one involving the order form. If we implement the proposed solution, who or what will be affected?"

Roland raised his hand and Dr. Elbie called on him. Roland smiled because he knew this one. He said, "The sales department will be affected. We'll no longer need a full time secretary to do the transcription from one form to another."

"Excellent!" Dr. Elbie said. "As we categorize these wastes, the answers to who or what will be affected become apparent."

Buck was dozing off in the back of the room. Dr. Elbie looked his way and everyone else turned around. A few people began to smile as Dr. Elbie continued, "For instance, if we elect to farm out our expediting operation, Mr. Grimes can eliminate his shipping department."

Buck awoke just as he said that. He yelled, "No one is going to close down my department! You do that and you and your bloody horse are dead meat!"

Dr. Elbie smiled at Mr. Grimes and then responded, "You know, Buck, I think everyone in here would agree with you, and believe me, I wouldn't suggest any such thing. I guess I was just testing that sixth sense of yours. Apparently it's working OK. Did you have a good sleep?"

Buck was a little embarrassed and apologized for dozing off. "My baby girl was up all night. I'm sorry."

Dr. Elbie admitted, "By the way, Buck, I was teasing you just then. I'm also sorry for interrupting your snooze, but I would like to restate a point that we made earlier. Several people have approached me in the halls and out in the shop. There will be no lay-offs as a result of this training. There may be significant changes in some people's jobs, but we'll try to anticipate those changes to insure a smooth transition to a new work environment.

"OK, let's get started here. I'm going to list three categories of waste. They're probably the three biggest wastes in any company. These are the waste of human potential, the waste of rework (or bad quality parts) and the waste of waiting. We actually have twelve categories of waste. We will cover those later, but for now, let's just look at these three.

"As we go on, wastes that fall into these three specific categories will be the lion's share of those we find. You're going to create categories for the ones that don't fit into one of these three and then we'll compare your categories with those that we've collected. The reason we do it this way is to force you into a new way of looking at the processes in this plant and work in general.

"As I bring other associates in to work with you, we aren't going to figure out your problems and solutions for you. The value that we add to this company is to guide you in the way that you think for yourselves.

"I suppose that I could bring in some other consultants, like CNC machine tool wizards and cost accountants. We could come in and do the things that you want us to implement. Do you know what would happen?

"After we did all the work, we would be the ones who learned about your business during the implementation process. Guess what would probably happen?"

Jim had not really been talkative; now he reacted to Dr. Elbie's comments. He said, "You mean that you aren't going to help us?"

"No, Jim, that's not what I said. I said that we are not going to do the implementations, you are. We'll help you by keeping you focused on your goals and supplying any resources that you need. The sooner you learn to do this, the quicker you'll be able to stand alone and not require our help. If we don't get you independent as quickly as possible, you people will be like the proverbial bull in a china shop. And more than likely, you won't be any better off than before.

"You're the ones who need to create a new culture. You're the ones who are going to live with it, so you're the ones who have to create it. I really believe that your collective intellect is a powerful resource to apply to a problem. In just about every successful project that I have worked on over the last twenty years, the common theme for all of them is this: *Simpler is better.*

"The late, great jazz musician Charlie Mingus had a better way of saying it.

> Anybody can make the simple complicated.
> Creativity is making the complicated simple.

"The primary focus of this training is to get you to accomplish three things:

1. To think for yourselves
2. To take responsibility for your own jobs
3. To learn to work with each other as a team.

"OK, we've got about twenty minutes left in this class. I want you to take the wastes that we listed and categorize them. Would someone please volunteer to take notes?"

Jim's hand went up and Dr. Elbie said, "Great, Jim. Would you please keep track of the list of the various categories and the wastes that we identify? We will post the results daily."

So we went to work on the list of wastes. Everyone had ideas. Jim had a pretty hard time keeping up with all the stuff that was being thrown at him, but somehow he managed. I thought we got some pretty good results.

7

The next morning Dr. Elbie handed out mimeographed sheets of the wastes and their categories. It was a large list that had been collected from all the different classes. Our class had thirty-seven wastes listed and seven classifications. Most of the other classes were in the same range. A lot of our wastes were duplicated in other classes.

Then I looked at the sheet from the fifth class of the day. They had listed seventy-nine wastes and twelve categories! That class was made up of mostly women from the quality and testing area.

Gus looked at the same list and started to laugh. "They probably suggested what color to paint the john," he said.

I was looking at the list and they had some good stuff on it. They had a category called Waste of Poor Planning, and at the top of that was Waste of Having to Work Unscheduled Overtime.

Man, this was heavy duty! We examined the list pretty closely.

Dr. Elbie started off, "Today we're going to talk about the topic of teams at length. Incidentally, does anyone have an idea why the fifth class is knocking the stuffing out of the rest of you guys?"

Nobody said anything, but everyone looked pretty irritated. So Dr. Elbie continued, "The reason that they're doing so well is that, for the most part, they already know how to work as a team. By the very nature of their job, they've been forced to learn to rely on each other's expertise and suggestions when they are running tests or troubleshooting."

As Dr. Elbie spoke, I thought about my experiences working with other people. My dad and I had worked as a team in that little shop in his garage. We talked about how we were going to do various projects and we solved problems together. He taught me just about everything I knew and he still asked for my advice.

Dr. Elbie was serving that same function here. He was a teacher, but he was also working with us to discover our problems, giving us problem solving techniques and getting us to present our solutions to the class. He was teaching us to look at the work we did in a different way. He didn't know how to make our work better, *we* did. He was giving us the tools.

When I worked as an apprentice, the journeymen and I formed a team. It was pretty informal. We were assigned jobs and as we worked together, I learned. After I became a journeyman, I sometimes worked with an apprentice.

At Osgood's we had teams of sorts. Everyone knew each other. Parents, sons and daughters were all working in the same plant. But we weren't really teams.

I guess I wasn't sure what a team was.

After I learned the computer programming for the CNC, I taught it to a couple of other people and we all did the programming, but we did it individually. We each came up with our own solutions to whatever problems we had. We worked together and shared ideas, but we weren't really a team. Something was missing.

When Osgood sold the company, any idea of teamwork went right out the window. Even Charlie, who loved being a machinist, and freely shared his knowledge and experience, got to the point where he just ran his machine and collected his paycheck.

Dr. Elbie told us there already was a team operating in the plant. It made sense when he told us that they were beating us to the punch. They had organized themselves in a way that made them a team and they were good. They communicated well and no egos were evident.

That department was able to keep up with any amount of work that we could throw at them. They were very efficient. Dr. Elbie had mentioned that to me when I first met him. He told me that factories organized as teams were not just a little more efficient, they were a lot more efficient than traditional plants.

Dr. Elbie was at the board again. He wrote BASEBALL in big block letters. "What do you think of when you see this word?" he asked rhetorically. "You think of a baseball team. You may think of an individual player if he's been getting a lot of press lately, but mostly you think of a team. Well, a baseball team is no different than any business or factory team. Let me explain.

"On any baseball team there are teams within teams, and support teams outside of the team that takes the field. All of these groups are required as support for the team that takes the field.

"The front office team handles everything from player trades and contract negotiations to new stadium proposals. They're the ones who deal with the lawyers when someone is hit by a foul ball. And they worry about making money in the concessions. They're concerned with the difficult logistics of moving eighty players, coaches and support personnel around the country.

"On the playing field there are individual teams, the battery of the pitcher and catcher, the combination of shortstop and second base. Outfielders have ways of communicating with each other that only they know. During the game, sometimes there are teams that only exist for a moment. The pitcher might make a snap throw to second base, but we've all seen enough balls end up in the outfield to know this is not effective team building.

"So who adds value on a baseball team?" He paused for a second but there was no reply. Then he said, "Only the players on the field, but all the other people involved are essential for those players to be able to play.

"This plant is exactly like that baseball team. The executive offices here negotiate contracts, buy insurance, order raw materials. They design new products and work with finance and marketing to bring these new products to market.

"Who adds value in this company? The people who make the products, the machinists and assemblers who are essential to getting the product out the door. Does a pinch hitter add value when he is sitting on the bench? The answer is obvious: he only adds value when he's at the plate taking his cuts. It's the same in this business. Just as the pinch hitter needs the manager to tell him when to go in, the people here who actually add value need the rest of the support people in order to do their jobs."

As Dr. Elbie spoke, I thought about the way that Quality Pump worked. It seemed that all the departments were autonomous and that there wasn't a hell of a lot of communication between them. It was obvious that we didn't have any teams. When there was communication, everyone was trying to blame someone else. There was very little cooperation among the various departments.

The example from class yesterday when we found that the sales order was wrong was typical of what happened at Quality Pump. We catered to employees' egos, and, as a result, the customer was not properly serviced. As I thought about these issues, I couldn't help but recall a question Dr. Elbie had asked in class several days ago: *How much waste in American Business is due to management structures that do not encourage teamwork?*

What Dr. Elbie said made sense. I liked playing on different teams. I liked playing high school football, basketball and baseball. I liked playing on Osgood's softball team. But I really didn't understand how teams generate more profitable business. Why was a team more profitable than individually managed organizations?

Maybe it had to do with organization and waste elimination. Maybe I would see it later. I always liked to be with my teammates. We were part of a team and we competed against other teams. We suffered together and celebrated together. In a company, teams are there to service customers. They compete with teams at other companies. In a way, that was what he was talking about. If everyone works together and there is no blame for failure, then everyone can communicate and we can continue to improve our work. Maybe that's what this was about.

When I worked with my dad, our two heads were better than one. Perhaps we could work in the plant like I worked with my dad.

8

By the end of the first week of class, we all realized that Quality Pump was in a world of trouble. One of the main things that became clear to everyone was that our problems weren't just on the shop floor. They were everywhere.

If Bonnie or Mr. Diamond were out of the office when an order came in, the order might get lost for days at a time. There was lots of money at risk for Mr. Grimes because many of the lost orders had penalties for late delivery. And we always seemed to be late.

The sales department was sloppy, accounting was incompetent, production was inefficient, engineering had no clue and the shipping and receiving area was in a fog.

During the first week, we found that the purchasing department took ninety-five steps to get a purchase order through the system. One of the other classes had figured the cost of lost time in processing such an order and it was terrible. It was over two hundred dollars in wasted time on our part and that of the supplier.

Mr. Grimes almost went crazy when he looked at these problems. How was he going to get out of this mess? It seemed that our left hand didn't know what our right hand was doing. Mr. Grimes had put his heart and soul into this business and it was being torn apart in front of him daily in the classes. One day he would see light at the end of the tunnel and the next day another problem would come up that he didn't know about. Everyone knew that this was not an easy time for Mr. Grimes. He had to eat crow and we weren't providing any catsup. Dr. Elbie said this at the beginning: During the VAP process, it is OK to provide catsup to the boss while he is eating crow.

Everyone liked Mr. Grimes now and we hated to see him suffer from our ideas. It made sense that he wouldn't like the input, but he was enduring it all with great courage.

I talked with Gus and some other guys and was told that Mr. Grimes had started Quality Pump in an office across town. Apparently, Mr. Grimes had a degree in mechanical engineering and had started to rep pumps for a small pump manufacturer. During the early days he had to repair pumps as they failed in the field. When he got them back in the shop, he noticed that most of the pumps were failing for the same reason. Being a gifted engineer, he redesigned the lower end of the pump where the bearing and shaft assembly came together. A patent was issued to him and Quality Pump was born. He started in a small building and quickly outgrew it.

Then Mr. Grimes bought a large piece of property outside of town where he built the current plant. The plant had been remodeled and expanded a couple of times over the last forty years, but it certainly wasn't the most efficient layout. As one of the guys pointed out, it felt like Mr. Grimes had used a crazed rat to help him in the design of the additions. Most of us agreed with that.

Mr. Grimes had expanded the plant without any real master plan. The expansions were usually forced on him by an unexpected order that extended over a long period of time or a new client with strong potential. Whatever the reasons for the layout, it was clearly very wasteful. Sometimes we had to move the work all around the shop to get it done.

In analyzing the layout, we identified a new category of waste. We called it the Waste of Poor Plant Layout. Dr. Elbie told us this waste was actually two separate wastes. One was the Waste of Building and Equipment and the other was Waste of Poor Planning.

It became apparent as Dr. Elbie worked with us that the whole business was like the plant. We found a lot of processes and paperwork that generated waste. They might have made sense when they were put in place, but now they were just dragging the whole business down.

Our class alone had now come up with seventy different wastes. We broke them down as follows:

Class 1
VAP WASTES

Waste of:
1. not having the right tools (inspection and processing)
2. inspection
3. mishandling—damage, dings and scratches
4. handling
5. over-finishing
6. looking for misplaced items
7. shift change
8. not knowing next job

9. looking for time card
10. bad plating process
11. generating wasted paperwork
12. repeating verbal order that wasn't written down
13. not having knowledge of available tools
14. pathways through shop
15. waiting for next job
16. not having setup ready—manual & CNC
17. not having materials with job
18. cleaning work area left dirty
19. waiting for instructions & waiting for manager
20. too many meetings
21. cleaning up after previous shift
22. not documenting change of setup
23. scrap and rework
24. waiting for first articles
25. running to tool store
26. looking for traveller
27. not putting tools away
28. maintenance being done by machinists
29. not using machines to their capabilities (run 35% to 70%)
30. making phone calls
31. waiting for engineering change
32. setup (optimum setup time is zero)
33. idle machines
34. going for coffee
35. looking for carts
36. cramped, inefficient shop layout
37. loading parts
38. leaving machines on
39. timekeeping (twenty minutes per person)
40. lack of leadership (many opinions on job problem resolution)
41. not enough tooling material
42. not having fixtures for all jobs
43. inadequate tool magazine capacity
44. waiting for tools
45. delivering parts to clients
46. moving WIP work around shop
47. bad planning for meetings (beginning & end of day)

48. having payroll clerk
49. supervisors
50. waiting for/sharing inspection equipment
51. having preliminary production job from main shop
52. carrying inventory
53. one computer per machine
54. having to move things to get to work area
55. loading parts by hand (too heavy and dangerous)
56. carrying bar stock by hand
57. looking for tools
58. having band saw a distance from production
59. machining parts to tighter tolerances than required
60. crashing tools
61. putting unqualified people on jobs
62. over-deburring
63. deburring at machine & deburring later
64. repairing the tumbler
65. rushing other workers
66. electrical outlets and hoses in wrong places (too short)
67. incorrect tooling sheets
68. omissions of what's controlled on tooling sheets
69. lost creativity due to stress
70. doing work out of sequence

After the wastes were sized, the above list looked like:

Class 1
VAP CATEGORIZED WASTES

After the first class in sizing & categorizing the wastes, they broke down as follows (At the end of the class several wastes had not yet been assigned to categories):*

1. Waste of Human Potential   COST

20. too many meetings $131,000

---

* The reader may not agree with the way that these wastes are assigned but it is done with consensus and if the workers and employees feel that the waste is properly placed in a particular category, then so be it.

47. bad planning for meetings (beginning
    & end of day) $131,000
39. timekeeping (twenty minutes per
    person) $ 50,000
11. generating useless paperwork $ 44,000
49. supervisors $ 43,750
27. not putting tools away $ 36,000
21. cleaning up after previous shift $ 31,250
34. going for coffee $ 31,000
12. repeating verbal order that wasn't
    written down $ 30,333
22. not documenting change of setup $ 18,750
40. lack of leadership (many opinions on
    job problem resolution) $ 13,750
18. cleaning work area left dirty $ 12,500
60. crashing tools $ 3,475
9. looking for time card $ 1,625
61. putting unqualified people on jobs   ?

2. Waste of Overproduction

19. waiting for instructions & waiting for
    manager $151,000
7. shift change $ 84,000

3. Waste of Waiting

26. waste of waiting for traveller $106,000
33. idle machines $ 75,000
15. waiting for next job $ 46,000
24. waiting for first articles $ 28,000
30. making phone calls $ 6,250
31. waiting for engineering change $ 4,800

4. Waste of Transportation/Handling

3. mishandling—damage, dings and
    scratches $ 41,666
4. handling   ?
45. delivering parts to clients $ 35,000

5. Waste of Process/Methods

2. inspection	$495,000
32. setup (optimum setup time is zero)	$117,000
5. over-finishing	$ 84,000
59. machining parts to tighter tolerances than required	$ 75,000
42. not having fixtures for all jobs	$ 13,000
37. loading parts	$ 6,500
17. not having materials with job	$ 3,200

6. Waste of Motion

6. looking for misplaced items	$130,000
14. pathways through shop	$ 37,500
25. running to tool store	$ 6,250
46. moving WIP around shop	$ 5,208
56. carrying bar stock by hand	$ 625
57. looking for tools	$ 800

7. Waste of Stock

52. carrying inventory	$ 17,000

8. Waste of Design

9. Waste of Poor Quality

23. scrap and rework	$ 30,000+
10. bad plating process	$ 15,000

10. Waste of Facilities/Equipment

29. not using machines to their capabilities (run 35% to 70%)	$400,000
50. waiting for/sharing inspection equipment	$ 32,500
1. not having the right tools (inspection and processing)	$ 32,000

13. not having knowledge of available
    tools $ 31,250
36. cramped, inefficient shop layout $ 20,000
35. looking for carts $ 16,750
43. inadequate tool magazine capacity $ 7,500
38. leaving machines on $ 1,800
53. one computer per machine   ?
55. loading parts by hand (too heavy and
    dangerous)   ?

11. Waste of Complexity

48. having a payroll clerk   ?

12. Waste of Planning

16. not having setup ready (manual &
    CNC) $ 43,750
28. maintenance being done by machin-
    ists $ 12,000
8. not knowing next job $ 6,250
44. waiting for tools $ 3,125
41. not enough tooling material $ 1,250
51. having preliminary production job
    from main shop   ?
54. having to move things to get to work
    area   ?
58. having band saw a distance from
    production   ?

UNASSIGNED WASTES—The class didn't finish these. It is left as an exercise for the reader to figure out where these wastes belong.

62. over-deburring
63. deburring at machine & deburring
64. repairing the tumbler
65. rushing other workers

66. electrical outlets and hoses in wrong places (too short)
67. incorrect tooling sheets
68. omissions of what's controlled on tooling sheets
69. lost creativity due to stress
70. doing work out of sequence

On Monday morning I walked into class a few minutes before seven. A few guys were standing around, looking at the bulletin board. I joined them and saw the usual stuff on the board: the lists of wastes from each class, a No Blame poster on which somebody had handwritten the word REMEMBER. Tacked on the middle of the board was a handwritten memo from Mr. Grimes that said:

WASTE REDUCTION IS OUR NUMBER ONE GOAL!!!

Buck stood next to me, saw the memo and laughed. "Boy, isn't this a trip," he said. "It's just like all the other rockets that Mr. Grimes launches. First, it was Quality Circles. Then it was Statistical Process Control. Now this." He pointed to the bulletin board. "I really like what we're doing but I get a strong feeling that it's just another one of those rockets."

Buck was pretty hard to ignore. He knew Mr. Grimes very well. I had been afraid this was going to be like all the other programs too, but for some reason, I didn't have that feeling now.

Mr. Grimes and Roland came in and sat down. Precisely at 7:00, Dr. Elbie entered the classroom. "Good morning," he said. "I trust we all had a restful weekend?"

Tony said, "You ruined mine."

Dr. Elbie looked surprised and asked, "How's that, Tony?"

Tony pulled out a sheaf of papers and said, "I couldn't get to sleep Friday night. All the stuff that we'd been talking about in class kept running around in my head. I went to bed early because I was going hunting in the morning, but I couldn't get to sleep.

"I got up and tried to make some sense out of that damn list of wastes. By the time I got to bed, it was late. I think I hit the sack around 3:30 in the morning.

"Saturday morning I got up too late to go hunting, so I spent the whole weekend trying to come up with some solutions for our problems. My wife thinks I'm crazy. She says I'm just a damn machinist and I ought to leave well enough alone."

"Well," Dr. Elbie replied, "in a way, she's right. You are a machinist. More importantly, you really believe that you can make a difference. Everybody does. The reason these classes are such powerful stimulants is that they make you realize that everyone's job is on the line. You *should* be worrying about things we discuss in this class. I'm glad I ruined your weekend. I think with that kind of enthusiasm and ingenuity the problems in this company will be overcome."

Dr. Elbie paused a moment and then addressed the class. "Did anyone else have a weekend like Tony?"

About 80% of the class, including me, raised their hands. I had spent the weekend trying to do a better layout for the area where we make the valve bodies.

Dr. Elbie was excited. "EXCELLENT!" he shouted. "Later on in the week we are going to break up into teams and work on some of these opportunities for improvement. These teams will be assigned a project responsibility to find $100,000 of waste which can be fixed for a cost of less than $5,000. In about 2 weeks, you will then be asked to make a presentation to management. We'll spend more time on this later. So keep your ideas coming." With that he walked to the board and wrote the words PROCESS Map. "Today we're going to talk about process, but not just on the shop floor. We are going to talk about what happens from the time an order is placed until the product is shipped to the customer. We're not going to stop measuring the process there. We're going to go on to another major event in the sales process. It follows the shipment of the product to the customer. It is the most important thing that occurs in any business. Does anyone have any idea what I am referring to."

So far, Roland had not volunteered much during the class. He seemed to be above participating with us unless his department was being attacked and then he would go on the defensive.

Now Roland decided to jump into the discussion. "Dr. Elbie," he said, "I think that what you are looking for is the shipment of the invoice with the order."

Dr. Elbie looked at Roland for a second and said, "Does everyone agree with him?"

Nobody said anything. Then Buck jumped in. "Like you said earlier, Dr. Elbie, the most important thing that our customers do after

The New Turnaround

receiving our pumps is send us money. Cold hard cash. No checks please." Everyone in the class chuckled at Buck's lighthearted response.

Dr. Elbie stood near where Mr. Grimes was seated. Mr. Grimes was a little upset at Buck's breezy attitude. Dr. Elbie said, "I don't know what anyone else thinks, but I think he's got it! Buck understands that Rule Number One in business is: GET PAID! I am not joking. It is very important to send a bill. And I also agree with Roland, you must start there. That's why Accounts Receivable is so important. If they do their job right and they collect in a timely manner from your customers, you'll survive.

"Too many companies isolate sales from collections. Sales people keep taking orders from customers that have a problem paying." Dr. Elbie moved near Roland as he said this and was talking to him as if no one else was in the room.

Roland jumped up and said, "Are you implying that we are taking orders from flakes, that we're giving this stuff away?"

Dr. Elbie responded, "I really don't know anything about any of your customers. What is the current value of accounts receivable?"

Roland sat down. He looked at Mr. Grimes, who nodded his head. Roland said, "I don't have exact figures, but it's probably about $1.9 million, give or take."

Dr. Elbie then looked at Mr. Grimes and inquired if that figure was accurate. Mr. Grimes responded sharply, "It's $2.83 million exactly, not giving or taking anything."

Mr. Grimes seemed angry that Mr. Diamond did not know the exact answer. He knew that accounts receivable was very important to the success of his business. Dr. Elbie had clearly set Roland up for that situation. I wondered why he would do such a thing. Then I wondered who else he would set up. After all, nobody likes to be embarrassed.

The room was quiet. Dr. Elbie smiled at Mr. Grimes and walked over to me. He looked at me and asked, "How long did your last setup take?" The question caught me a little off-guard, but since I had kept records as Dr. Elbie had asked, I had the answer. I replied, "Six hours and thirty-five minutes."

As he walked to the front of the room he said, "Good. Roland, I'm sorry that I picked on you, but I wanted to make a point. As we go forward, we're going to have to rethink all the numbers that we report to management. We want everyone in the company to be measured by numbers that they use in the daily performance of their job.

"For example, I just asked over there," pointing to me, "about his most recent setup. He knew the status of his work performance from yesterday. That's what we're going to do for everyone. It's important to know *what* you are doing, but more important than anything, you want to know *how* you're doing. Does everyone understand this principle?"

Buck jumped right in. "Yeah, I understand perfectly. You want us to play the game and know what the score is. I can get behind that. I never did like playing games where the score was a mystery. You never know if you're winning or losing."

Mr. Grimes turned in his chair and said to Buck, "You know, Buck, you just cleared up something that nobody has been able to explain to me before. Now I understand that if you play the game, you don't want to know the score weeks or months later. Nobody wants to play that game, but that's what we ask you to do all the time." He turned to face Dr. Elbie. "Jack, I think we all understand. That's great! Let's keep going."

Dr. Elbie went to the easel, and started to draw a series of squares and bubbles on the easel paper. As he worked, he said, "We call this technique a Process Map. We'll map the process required to get an order into the system, manufactured, shipped and the invoice paid. Are you all ready? Feel free to jump in any time with an observation or a comment, particularly if we miss any steps in the process."

I thought this was going to be boring, but I couldn't have been more wrong. Dr. Elbie wrote Customer in the middle of the right side of the easel paper and Bonnie raised her hand, "After I make a sale, I bring the order form to Beth, our secretary. She types it up on a work order, then we distribute five copies."

The New Turnaround

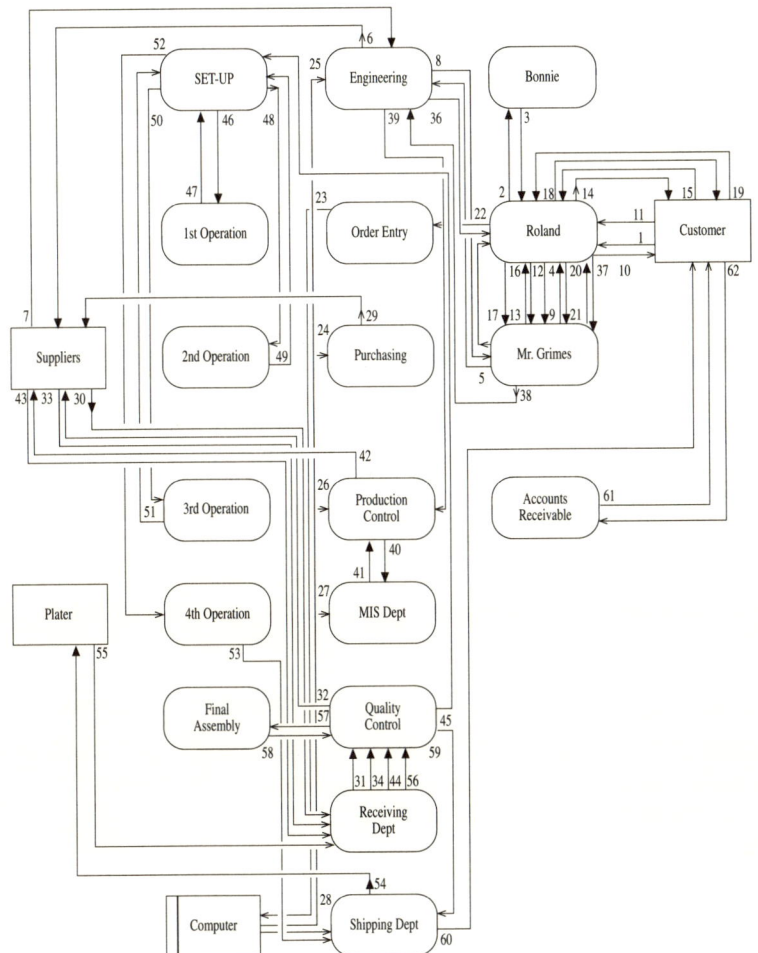

Process Map

1 Customer calls to discuss product
2 Roland refers action to Bonnie
3 Bonnie gets facts together and gives to Roland
4 Roland readjusts dollar amount and sends to Mr. Grimes
5 Mr. Grimes checks with engineering
6 Engineering calls various suppliers for quotes
7 Suppliers return quotes to engineering
8 Engineering notifies Mr. Grimes on quotes
9 Mr. Grimes approves order
10 Roland sends quote to customer
11 Customer changes mind and orders few items
12 Roland gets new quote prepared
13 Mr. Grimes approves it
14 Roland sends new quote to customer
15 Customer OK's quote and sends order with different ship date
16 Roland notifies Mr. Grimes of different ship date
17 Mr. Grimes doesn't approve

18 Roland gets acceptable ship date
19 Customer approves
20 Roland notifies Mr. Grimes of customer approval ship date
21 Mr. Grimes accepts order
22 Roland gives order to order entry
23 Order entry enters into computer
24 Copies given to purchasing
25 Copy to engineering
26 Copy to production control
27 Copy to MIS department
28 Copy to shipping
29 Purchasing orders material and schedules plaster
30 Materials delivered to receiving
31 Receiving delivers material to quality control, QC inspects
32 QC rejects some material
33 Vendor delivers replacement material
34 Receiving delivers material to QC
35 QC OK's all material and moves to stock room
36 Engineering prepares drawing changes
37 Roland reviews
38 Mr. Grimes approves changes
39 Drawings sent to production control
40 Production control schedules job in MIS system
41 MIS run delivered to production control
42 Production control orders tools and fixtures from tool and die shop
43 Tool and die returns complete tools and fixtures
44 Receiving delivers material to QC
45 QC inspects fixtures
46 Setup starts at first operation
47 **Run on first operation—value-added**
48 Setup on second operation
49 **Run on second operation—value-added**
50 Setup on third operation
51 **Run on third operation—value-added**
52 Setup on fourth operation
53 **Run on fourth operation—value-added**
54 Shipping trucks to plater
55 **Plater—value-added**
56 Products received at receiving
57 Move to QC, QC inspects plated parts
58 **Final assembly—value-added**
59 QC does final inspection
60 Ship to customer
61 Invoice sent
62 Customer pays

The New Turnaround

"OK, where do the copies go?" Dr. Elbie asked. As people responded, he wrote the names and places on the board and drew lines between them. He also numbered the lines and put arrows next to them to indicate which way the flow was going. People were talking and arguing among themselves and still giving instructions to Dr. Elbie. The board started to look like my daughter's Etch-a-Sketch after she had been playing with it all afternoon. Hashing out where all the paperwork went took almost the whole hour, but we finally got finished.

We looked at the Process Map and the lines drawn on it. There were several different steps. As Dr. Elbie counted up the trail, he wrote 62 MOVES on the board. Everyone was amazed. As we examined the Process Map we found that our process added value in only 6 of the 62 steps. In other words, 90% of the steps did not generate value.

"On the basis of this Process Map we can see that only 10% of your business operations actually add value," Dr. Elbie said. And then he went to the Process Map and drew green lines on the chart for those steps that added value.

What was great about this chart was that it allowed everyone to see the whole system. We could really see the inefficiency of it. We could see all those things that we do that don't add value.

Dr. Elbie talked briefly with Mr. Grimes, who got up and walked over to the Process Map. He stared at it for a few minutes and then turned to the class. "You want to know something? I am stupid. Dr. Elbie has been trying to tell me this for over a month. Now I see what he means." He turned back to the Process Map and said, "This is pretty bad. The fact that I let it get this bad is just plain stupid.

"Jack Prescott told me to be ready for the Process Map of my organization. I was sitting there quietly as the whole process of getting an order, shipping it and collecting for it was reviewed. Now I see that we really need help!"

He looked over at Dr. Elbie, who approached Mr. Grimes, and the two of them talked for a minute. Dr. Elbie nodded in agreement to something.

Mr. Grimes turned to the class and said, "I'll tell you what I'll do. It looks to me that each step on the Process Map that is eliminated will save me a bundle of money. For your help in eliminating these steps, I'll put one thousand dollars into a pool for every step in that process that is eliminated. We'll divvy it up every month equally among all the employees. That way, you all benefit. Is that a good deal, or what?"

Mr. Grimes was excited. He could see the value of the Process Map and was glad to encourage us to start eliminating the fifty-six non-value-adding steps. Interestingly Dr. Elbie explained that this tool is applicable to any production or control situation. It even applies to the paper flow in an insurance company, a bank or a hospital. You name it.

Mr. Grimes had taken over the lecture. "I really like this! Every one of these moves is an opportunity for error: from lost paperwork to a number that gets copied wrong. This monster was not created overnight. Each move made sense to someone when it was put in place, but when we look at the system as a whole it doesn't make sense." As he walked away from the front to sit down, Mr. Grimes looked over at Dr. Elbie and said, "Please go on, this is fun."

"I agree with you, John. It is fun. And we're going to improve the profits while we're having fun." Mr. Grimes nodded his head in total agreement.

Dr. Elbie continued, "OK, I wanted all of you to see how this happens. During the rest of the training, we're going to use this Process Map as a tool to get real answers to the problems in this company.

"So I hope this discussion provides all of you with something additional to think about. Look around while you're out there doing your job. Look for all the ways we can eliminate steps in the Process Map and we'll talk about them in class tomorrow."

The class was dismissed. Everyone was talking as the class left. I walked down the hall to the water cooler. As I bent over to drink, I happened to look down the hallway toward the offices. Roland was giving Dr. Elbie the business. He was mad about being embarrassed in class.

I walked back to my machine. Tony came over and grabbed me. He said, "You know what? I'm really surprised at myself. I usually don't like these kinds of classes, but I like this one. I think that we're getting to the real problems. You know, I think this guy might be different. For some reason, though, it looks like Dr. Elbie thinks that Roland is a problem. I wonder what he really knows and why he picked on Roland today."

I didn't think of it that way. I figured that he was trying to get Roland to rethink what he was doing. It was pretty clear that Roland and Mr. Grimes were not communicating very well. Roland didn't know the value of accounts receivable, which was something Mr.

Grimes thought he should know to the penny and have on the tip of his tongue.

I had met Roland on several occasions since being at Quality Pump and I liked him. Roland was a nice guy. Tony was still feeling concerned about Roland.

He went on ". . . but we need better communication with sales. I really don't know how to say it, but I think they don't give us enough information and that's one reason why there are so many mistakes."

9

The next morning Dr. Elbie popped a tape into the VCR. He said, "This morning we're going to talk some more about team building. We're going to touch on this subject throughout the training. Hopefully, by the time this training has ended, you'll all have a grasp of how and why a team works. You must all understand: WITHOUT EFFECTIVE TEAMWORK, NONE OF THESE IMPROVEMENTS WILL WORK! They may last for a few months but they will not be permanent. By the time we end this process of productivity improvement, you'll understand teams and teamwork. Your teams will be organized around the work that is to be performed by each team. Remember this definition:

WORK IS:
PLANNING
CONTROLLING
DOING.

"In your experience, who does the planning and controlling?"

Tony was really jazzed from the previous day. He said, "Everyone but the people who should. The people who actually do the work know what they're doing. If they tell us the work they want done, we can plan it and control it. We certainly know how to *do* it."

Buck said, "I understand where you're leading us but I don't understand what you mean by control." Dr. Elbie went to the board and wrote:

CONTROL IS:
MEASURING and then
ADJUSTING.

Then he asked if anyone had sailed on the ocean. A couple of people raised their hands. Dr. Elbie asked one of them if he had ever sailed out of the sight of land. The guy told him that he had. Dr. Elbie asked if he had steered the boat and he said that he had. Dr. Elbie then asked, "How did you find your way back?"

The guy said, "When we wanted to return, we just set a compass course and followed it until we sighted land."

"And what did you do when you sighted land?" Dr. Elbie asked.

"We looked at where we were in relation to where we wanted to go and made an adjustment," he replied.

"Exactly!" Dr. Elbie exclaimed. He looked at the class and said, "Does everyone follow what was just said? If you understand that, you know all there is to know about control. The compass course is your plan, and as you set your plan, and take your readings (measure against the plan), you can make adjustments as needed.

"Do you think you can run this business the same way you sail a boat? Can everyone in the company get a daily reading on whether they're on course or not?"

You could just tell that Buck wasn't going to let that one sit. He said, "Of course we'd like to go sailing. We'd like to do that every day. I can't think of a better way to spend my day."

"To be quite frank, Buck," Dr. Elbie said, "personally, I hate sailing. I can never relax out there. I used that analogy because I was told that there are a lot of sailors in this company. I think most of you can get the drift of my message."

Dr. Elbie was enjoying this discussion. A few of us laughed.

He went on, "As I see the current situation, we need to understand what jobs add value; how those jobs that add value are planned, controlled and performed, and how they're measured and improved upon. We'll need to do this for every job in the plant. The most important thing we really need to understand is whether the current jobs are the right ones."

As Dr. Elbie was talking, you could feel a lot of tension in the room. People didn't seem to understand what Dr. Elbie was saying.

Then Andrew, one of the engineers, asked rather matter of factly, "Are you implying that some people are going to lose their jobs? I distinctly remember you saying earlier that no one would lose his or her job as a result of the training. Am I confused or not?"

Dr. Elbie smiled and responded, "When Mr. Grimes and I had our first discussions about this training, he agreed not to lay off anyone as a result of the training.

"But we expect everyone's job to change. Some people will be doing jobs that are a lot different than their current ones. That I *will* guarantee."

Andrew was pretty disturbed. He wasn't buying it at all. He said, "I don't believe you one bit. How can we improve our productivity without laying off good people? I've worked at other plants and when they tried to do these things people got fired. It always happens! Always! How can you say all the stuff that you have been saying and mean it? All you are doing is setting false expectations for us!"

Dr. Elbie was quiet. He was very serious. He knew this was an important issue to resolve.

He looked at Andrew and began to speak in a very soft voice, "Andrew, I understand your concern. I believe you're not alone in that concern. Is that true?"

As he looked around the room, he got nods of agreement. "First of all, let me understand the other programs that you've been involved with in the past. Were they cost containment programs or productivity improvement programs?"

Andrew started to get a little hostile. "What difference does it make what you call it? My brother is a lawyer and he says, if it looks like a duck, and quacks like a duck, it's a duck. To me, this program sounds a lot like a sophisticated program to cut costs and people."

Dr. Elbie responded, "Andrew, I would like to get into the question that I asked you earlier. Was the program that you were involved with before a cost containment program? In other words, did the program only pay attention to the costs of running the business and disregard the revenue side of the equation? Did you ever get around to fixing the system or did you just try to cut the costs? You know, Andrew, you can improve profitability by increasing revenues, reducing costs or a little of both."

Andrew responded, "You know, Dr. Elbie, I really can't answer that because I wasn't involved in any of the decisions. I only remember them lining us up one day to fire us after we had just gotten some lecture about how to improve our operations."

Dr. Elbie replied, "One of the first impressions I get of what you are saying is that the program focused on cutting costs. You were not allowed to buy any things that you needed to help you run the business. You cut inventory, you cut supplies, you cut everything to the bone. Right?"

Andrew responded, "Yes, that's exactly what we did."

Dr. Elbie asked, "Did you ever get to do anything to change your job, so that you could be more efficient?"

"Oh, yes," Andrew responded, "we all got to look at our jobs; we filed reports on things to do to improve. We had a meeting where we discussed all these ideas. Everyone got excited, just like here. And then we all got the ax."

"Andrew, your timing with this input is quite good. I was ready to get into this discussion soon. So today is just fine." Dr. Elbie moved over to the center of the room and leaned against the table.

He said, "One of the greatest differences between the process that we're experiencing and the cost containment program you endured is this: *Mr. Grimes is involved.* Andrew, did you ever see the owner or chief executive of the previous company involved in any of your meetings about productivity?"

Andrew shook his head indicating a no to Dr. Elbie's question.

Dr. Elbie went to the board and wrote:

Tell me . . . and I will forget.
Show me . . . and I will remember.
Involve me . . . and I will understand.

He said, "I don't know who said this but I heard it a long time ago. And that's what we intend to do here—get everyone involved. Not just Mr. Grimes."

With this Dr. Elbie looked at Andrew and asked, "Did you ever get to implement any changes to improve productivity?"

Again, Andrew shook his head no. "And finally, do you believe that there are incompetent people working at Quality Pump?"

Andrew felt that he had been cornered. He knew it was a trap. Any answer he gave, he would be wrong.

Before he could answer, Dr. Elbie jumped in, "Andrew, I'm sure that there are incompetent people. I put you on the spot because all of us have probably thought that about this company at one time or another. There may be incompetent people all over the place and that may be the reason that the company is in trouble. Now, it's a reasonable thought to have.

"More than anything, I am willing to bet that if they are incompetent, they are so because they were not properly trained to do their jobs. They may well understand that it is a wasteful job and cannot tell anyone that it is. There could be any number of reasons why they are incompetent.

"In all the training and interaction with people that I have had with this process, we're always able to define new jobs that help focus on how and where the job adds value. We find that we can challenge every job in the operation, in the administration and in the whole company and ask the very simple question: Does this job add value? If not, is it an essential support function or is it waste? In other words, we ask the important question:

Are we doing the right work?

"It's not enough to simply make the job more efficient. Efficiency experts have been doing that for years.

"Once we have that question on the table, we can get into the other questions later. Do you see what I am saying, Andrew?"

Andrew was still puzzled. "I see what you are saying and I follow your logic, but I'm not able to see what makes this program different. How can you say that you won't have any firings? There have to be! There have to be a lot of them to turn this company around quickly. You have to stop the bleeding before it gets out of control. The easiest way to fix things in companies is to reduce head count. It's the American way! Cut personnel and lower your costs."

"I guess you have the Doubting Thomas Syndrome," Dr. Elbie said. "You know, you won't believe it unless you can see it. I don't know how to answer you other than to let you see what happens over the next several weeks.

"I would like you to be impressed. Maybe you will, maybe you won't, but I have great confidence in all of you that you will make it work. Is that fair?"

Andrew again agreed and said, "This Doubting Thomas is willing to make it happen. I guess I'm just cautious. I would hate to have anyone around this place hurt by false expectations of security. I like this approach but I also like to be careful. It might save everyone a lot of grief if the issue is on the table."

Mr. Grimes smiled at Andrew and asked Dr. Elbie if he could have the floor for a moment. Dr. Elbie stood back and Mr. Grimes began, "Andrew, I'm very impressed with your comments. I liked your approach. It was very professional." At that point everyone in the room

The New Turnaround

began to applaud spontaneously for Andrew's performance. He was visibly proud of Mr. Grimes's acknowledgment.

Mr. Grimes sat down and Dr. Elbie walked to the front of the classroom. "Andrew, I also appreciate what you just said. It took a lot of courage. And it was appropriate lead-in material for what we need to do next.

"As we move forward, we're going to examine all of the work done in the factory. We'll also be looking at the way paperwork is moved around the organization. We're going to look at each work location and how it is organized and we're going to ask again and again: *Is that the right work?*

"As we understand each work location and the technology associated with each location, we are going to need to know how we can control the work. How can we measure whether we're doing a good job or not?

Dr. Elbie turned and went to the board; he was thinking or maybe distracted. Something was bothering him. As he turned to face the class, he said, "OK, you're ready. Let's talk about measurement." He was very excited about this subject. You could see it in his eyes. He was more energized than any of us had seen him before.

He went to the board, picked up the marker and turned to the class. "You know, we've been doing this process for a number of years and the most important part of what we do is to teach you about measurement. We don't mean measurement in the traditional variety, we mean measurement that makes a difference in how we work.

"Let me ask you a question, Buck. How do you know that you've done a good job today? At the end of the day, how do you know?"

"I don't," Buck replied, "I do my job and at the end of the day, if no one has yelled at me, then maybe I've done a good job."

Everyone chuckled at that and Dr. Elbie shot back, "Wouldn't you like to know? I mean wouldn't you like to know when you have done a good job?"

Buck liked these exchanges with Dr. Elbie and responded smartly, "Yes, Dr. Elbie, I would like to know. And I bet you have something to show us, don't you?"

Dr. Elbie smiled, "Yes, I do, Buck. Would you like to find out?"

Again, Buck was laughing as he acknowledged the game, "Yes, I would, Dr. Elbie, why don't you tell us."

"I will with your support." Dr. Elbie turned to the board and wrote while he was talking, "There are two major ways that we like to measure:

Yes/No Charts and World Record Reports.

Yes/No Charts tell us when we need to modify a behavior, like coming in late or a truck not leaving on time. When you combine the No Blame philosophy with the Yes/No Charts you can start to modify behavior. Whereas the World Record Reports tell us about the process. We want to know immediately how we are performing a process and the World Record Reports continuously reminds us of how we are doing in relation to the best ever performance of a particular process. We report these records daily. This will give you the feedback you need to know that you are doing a good job."

Dr. Elbie stopped for a second and asked if there were any questions. Bonnie immediately raised her hand, "I see how the Yes/No Charts might work for something like whether the truck leaves on time, either it did or it didn't. And you report it, you use the red X to show that it was a No and a green zero to show that it was a Yes. I see that.

Day   1 2 3 4 5 6 7 8 9 10

Did the truck leave on time? X X 0 0 0 X . . .

But truck departures seem different than tardiness. Why use Yes/No Charts on behavior problems like people coming in late?"

Dr. Elbie asked the class, "Can anyone help Bonnie?"

Tony jumped in, "I don't understand why you want to measure behavior? Why don't you just measure the output of the group? Use that World Record Report or any other form of measure."

Dr. Elbie turned to Bonnie, "He's asking you a good question."

Bonnie responded, "We need everyone in our group to be here on time. Then we can start measuring our output. So, the behavior that we need to measure is Do people care about coming into work? We measure that by asking the question, Did everyone get here on time?" She hesitated a second, "Oh, I see, you will be measuring the behavior. But will this correct the behavior?" She looked at Dr. Elbie for help.

Tony jumped back in, "Why not measure the individuals? Did each

The New Turnaround

person get in on time? I think if you post that you'll modify behavior real quick."

Dr. Elbie replied, "Suppose you did put everyones name up. Would that help?"

Buck spoke up, "I see what you're getting at, if you measure the team's performance, and not the individual's performance, you may get the behavior that you want. I know I wouldn't want my name up there. But I know if I came in late, and it would effect the measurement of my team, I would be angry at myself for letting the team down. In that case, it would modify my behavior."

Mr. Grimes stood up, "Buck, I am really excited by what you said. It made an awful lot of sense." He then turned to Dr. Elbie, "Is that what you intend this Yes/No Chart to do? It makes sense. But I still don't see why you don't measure the individuals."

Buck had an answer and could hardly wait to respond, "That's what is effective about this, Mr. Grimes; you measure the team's performance and not the individual's. I guarantee this, if your behavior affects the way I'm being measured then we will have an attitude adjustment discussion." Everyone laughed. Buck was on a roll, "But suppose that we don't need to be here on time and it's all a bunch of bull. What do we do then?"

Dr. Elbie turned to the class, "Do any of you have any help for Buck?"

Bonnie responded, "I don't think this will work if everyone doesn't agree that being on time is important. We have that problem in my area and I think it is because one person doesn't believe that it is important to be here on time. Everyone else in our area thinks that this is important."

Dr. Elbie interrupted, "This is what teamwork is all about. You have to reach a consensus that it is important for all the team members to be there to do their jobs. Suppose someone is handling the sales interface with your East Coast reps. Does that person have to get in early? You have to really look at the work of your team. If the work that you have defined says you all need to start work on time then so be it. But if you can have flex hours and still get your job done, then maybe you are worrying about the wrong things. Maybe it really isn't important for everyone to come in at 8:00 A.M.. The only way that you will find out is to talk about it openly.

"Let me quickly go over World Record Reports so that you get the idea. As a quick aside, the reason that we got into this measurement form occurred several years ago. I was working with a client and I gave the workers a very difficult goal. They argued that the goal was impossible, but I began measurement anyway. As the measurement unfolded, the workers made phenomenal improvement in their performance and as they got closer to their goal they started to coast. They saw that they could hit the goal and then stopped pressing to improve.

"But I had noticed something about most workers; they love to break records. So we decided to make a game of it by setting up the World Record Reporting Process. Here is how it works. The first day you start, you record the performance of that day's output or whatever is being measured. You record that number and report it as 100% of the goal. That performance is now the world record. Every day's output is compared to that number and performance is noted. Whenever the previous record is exceeded, the performance is shown to be above 100%. So the record was broken. The reporting of data is simply the ratio of today's performance to the world record. In the case of sales, you want the sales volume to go up, so you want to see the reported sales number reflect that goal. However, in the case of setup, you want it to go down. So performance improvement is a smaller number, and again the numbers are reported to reflect that goal. Consider the following chart.

The New Turnaround

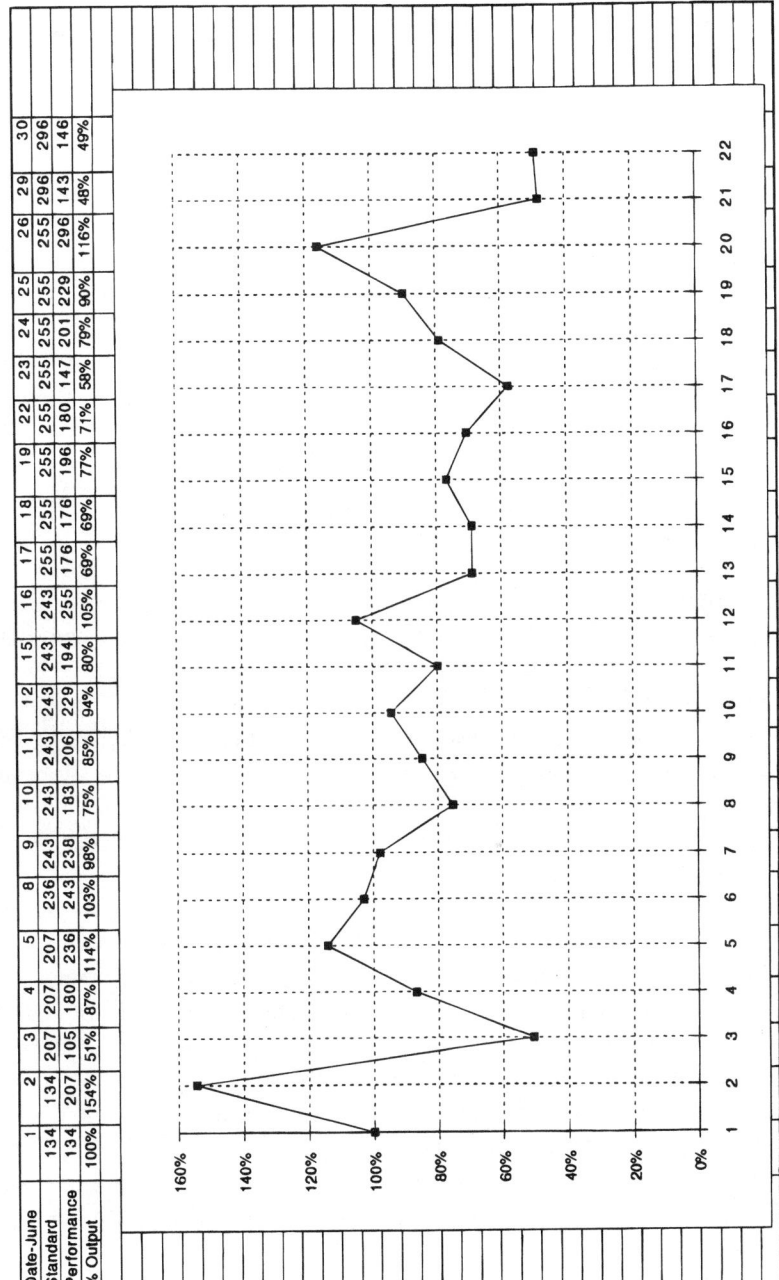

It shows a month's performance. The world record was broken five times during the month. The performance of daily output went from a world record of 134 to a world record of 296 on the twentieth day. The key to this is that the world record keeps going up and everyone is challenged to improve performance.

"This form of measurement is very important in continuous improvement environments because it shows clearly how often performance improves. We also think that posting the World Record Reports where they are visible to all is a good idea. So Mr. Grimes will be able to walk out to a particular work area and look at the World Record Report and know immediately if there is improvement. When he looks at the chart and sees no improvement in a month, he can ask what he can do to help. And that, my friends, is what measurement is all about. We will have ongoing discussions about measurement as we go along. Believe me, this is not the last you will hear about this.

"We need to make sure that the measures of all work are done on a timely basis! Does everybody understand this?"

Bonnie raised her hand. "Dr. Elbie, how can you look differently at the work we do in sales? It's always going to be the same: we talk to customers on the phone; we visit customers at their facilities; we take orders and we process them. How does our job change?"

Dr. Elbie looked at Bonnie and smiled. Then he looked at the class and asked, "Does anyone have any ideas about how Bonnie's job might change?"

You could tell immediately that Roland was visibly upset by what Bonnie had said.

At that point, Tony said matter of factly, "Bonnie, we showed earlier in the class how we can improve your order process with the new form. I also think that you could give us more of the information you get from customers about new products they might need or new features they want.

"I think we could all help you get new customers. We've never been involved with any of your customers and yet I think that they would be impressed by what we're doing here. I'm pretty excited about the project that we're working on. I think your customers would also be impressed and would like to do business with a company where everyone's involved.

"And you know what, Bonnie? I think that we would start appreciating you people in sales a lot more if you wouldn't isolate yourselves in your offices."

The New Turnaround

It looked like Dr. Elbie was amazed. Tony was very articulate. He was also very positive. Dr. Elbie began, "Tony, that was wonderful! Anyone have anything more to add?"

There was silence. Everyone was stunned!

Bonnie was clearly pleased by Tony's answer. I couldn't detect it, but I got the distinct feeling that Tony's response was not spontaneous. I thought that he and Bonnie were conspirators in something, but I never saw them together at work.

And then it clicked. They went to the same church. That was the only thing that I could key in on, but it made sense. They were trying to do something about improving the sales department.

From the look that Roland had given her earlier, it was clear that he did not approve of what Bonnie had asked.

The room was stirring a bit. Buck was dozing again in the back. Dr. Elbie had placed a cassette in the VCR player. He turned and said, "There are many ways of creating organizational conformity." Everyone shrugged their shoulders and looked around the room. Many heads were shaking.

Buck stirred. He said sleepily, "Say, what! Come on, Dr. Elbie! What the hell are you talking about?"

"OK, Buck," Dr. Elbie went on, "let's watch the tape and see if you would agree with this approach to team building. This is just one way of building a team. It may be similar to what Andrew experienced. You form your own opinions. As I said, it may not be the right way, but it is effective."

As Dr. Elbie started the tape, we saw a scene from the movie *The Untouchables* with Robert De Niro playing Al Capone. The men had just finished dinner and were sitting around a large round banquet table. Al Capone was lecturing the organization on team playing. He was talking about what it meant to be on his team. He said secrets were secrets. No one out of the circle of "associates" at the table was to be informed of any team-related activities. Al was holding a baseball bat and proceeded to give a negative demonstration of what happened to players who violated the sacred rules of his team. He hit one of his players with the bat several times.

As the tape ended, Dr. Elbie asked, "Would any of you want to play on his team. Certainly, that's one way to assure you have team players. It is a ruthless and vicious way of dealing with people. I showed that because American managers do pretty much the same thing to people who play on their teams. They have no idea how to create a team, but they sure know how to intimidate people."

He stopped and asked, "Does intimidation have anything to do with teams? What makes for an effective team? How does it get formed? Who should organize a team? How are teams organized? Who is on a work team? How do smaller teams interact with larger teams? What happens if someone doesn't want to be on a team?"

One of the engineers had been taking notes during the whole class. He hadn't said anything at all up to this point. Suddenly out of nowhere, he blurted out, "Slow down, Dr. Elbie. I can't keep up with you."

Dr. Elbie apologized and asked his name. He said, "Charles Shrensker, sir." He was almost military in his response. It was clear that he had been in a military organization. He was very stiff and never talked with anyone in the company.

Dr. Elbie called on Gus, who said, "My guys have been talking a lot about this team stuff. We all think that the tool and die guys are sort of a team already and that we shouldn't have to belong to any other teams."

Others in the class started to protest. Dr. Elbie raised his hands for silence. "I'll handle this," he said.

He walked around behind the desk at the front of the room and bent down. When he stood up, he was holding a Louisville Slugger. It was just like the one Al Capone was holding in the movie. As Dr. Elbie began swinging the bat, he looked straight at Gus and said, "We have ways of encouraging teamwork." Everyone laughed.

Dr. Elbie put the bat down and said "Hold it! This is not a joke. For a moment, let's just accept Gus's idea that they *are* a team unto themselves. Let's see how well that would work.

"On the face of it, it appears that we have at least one more communication requirement. This is an additional opportunity for error. It also slows down setup and puts too many people in positions of control. Who else has any ideas on how well this would work?"

I asked what he meant by too many people in positions of control. Dr. Elbie explained that in every situation someone has to make the final decision on how the work is scheduled and how it gets done. He went on to say that if Gus's team was autonomous, no matter what the other teams said, Gus's team would schedule their own work as they saw fit.

Dr. Elbie said, "A point of control occurs when there exists any person or group that can start or stop production and scheduling. It isn't very complicated. If I am the one who can start all classes, I am the point of control. If you can start a job in your area and Gus can do the same thing, unless you have phenomenal communications between you, you get a problem called *multiple points of control*. It is called that because more than one person can control a single job. Do you see that?" It was clear to me. That afternoon in the shop we got a real lesson on multiple points of control.

After class was over that morning Billy put me to milling parts for the control bodies. I was almost finished with the setup when Jim and Billy came over to my machine. Jim said, "I need you to do another job. It's a rush order so start setting up for it." He showed me a blue copy of a work order and Billy had the list for the setup.

Billy told me to get Gus and start setting up so that when the parts came back from the plater, we'd be ready. I went to find Gus to get the setup going. I told Gus what we needed to do and that it was a rush. He immediately stopped what he was doing and went to get the tools and jigs for the setup. I went back to my machine and started tearing down the previous job.

Although we didn't know it at the time, Mr. Grimes had gone to see Tony with the pink copy of the same work order. Whenever Mr. Grimes needs something expedited, he gets Tony to do it. He found him and said it was a rush order and to put somebody on it right away. Tony went back to the tool crib to look for Gus, but he wasn't there. So Tony told Frank to do it instead, and that he should get on it immediately.

As Tony walked away, Gus came out from the back of the tool crib. Gus had most of the setup completed and only needed a few more things to measure the offsets to complete the program. Before he left to get the other tools, he pushed his cart over by the coordinate measuring table. While Gus was getting his other tools together in the tool crib, Frank was doing the setup for Tony. He walked past Gus's cart. On the cart was a 16" center lube boring bar. The company only had two of them. They were custom made and by having two, we could work with one and send the other out for sharpening. The boring bar was *only used for this specific job*, so as he passed by, Frank grabbed the bar and went on his way.

When Gus brought the rest of his tools back to his cart, he set the tools down and noticed that the boring bar was missing. He scratched his head and muttered, "I know I had that son of a bitch on there," as he wandered back to the tool crib. He went back to where the bar was kept to see if he had forgotten it, but it wasn't there.

He came out to see me and asked, "Did you pick up that sixteen-inch boring bar? I can't find it."

I told him I hadn't seen it and he said, "This is crazy! I know I put it on the cart and now it's gone. We can only use it on this one job." He was shaking his head as he walked away.

Frank was measuring the offsets for his tools. He was hunched over the boring bar measuring the offset in its holder. Gus looked at him as he walked by, but didn't pay any attention to what Frank was doing. He walked back to the tool crib again and asked a couple of men if they had seen the bar; they said they hadn't.

Gus got frustrated easily and this was starting to get to him. He knew he had put the boring bar on the cart. He looked around for a while longer and then went to see Jim.

"Jim," he said, "do you know what happened to that boring bar for this setup? I had it on my cart and when I went back it wasn't there. I can't find it anywhere. It just disappeared."

Jim replied, "I haven't seen it. Don't we have another one?" Gus explained that there were only two and that the other one was at the sharpening shop. Jim said, "Well, we don't have time to fool around. Send somebody over to the sharpener to get the other one." Gus went off in search of a driver.

Tony's crew was almost finished with the setup, so Tony went off to find Bernard to have him input the program. When the driver got back with the boring bar from the sharpener, Gus quickly took the offset, dropped off the boring bar with me, and went into Bernard's office.

Gus asked Bernard to drop what he was doing and run this program. Bernard told him that the program he was entering was a rush order from Tony and that as soon as he was finished with it he would start on Gus's. Gus stood and fumed as Bernard finished. Gus handed the work order to Bernard and Bernard said "I just entered this program for Tony's cell! Are you sure this is the right work order?"

Man, you could hear the yelling all the way down the hall, even over the sound of the machines! Gus was a funny sight, yelling and waving the blue work order in the air, but no one was laughing.

Gus grabbed Jim and me and we walked over to Tony's cell. They were just finishing the same setup that we had been working on. Gus said, "Tony, what the hell is going on? Jim gave *me* this setup."

The New Turnaround

Tony said, "How should I know? Mr. Grimes came down here right after class and told me this was a rush order and to get right on it!"

"Look!" Gus said, "There's the damn boring bar I was looking for! Who took it?" Frank said that he had found it on a cart and just put it with his stuff. It looked like Gus and Frank were going to get into a fight. Jim stepped in between the two and calmed things down.

Just then, Mr. Grimes walked over to where we were. I guess he heard all the commotion. "What the hell is this, a convention?" he said.

Jim explained to him what had happened. Mr. Grimes said that it was his fault for not checking with Jim before having Tony start the job. Mr. Grimes said, "Well, at least the setup's done, so let's start running these parts."

"We can't. The parts aren't back from the plater," Jim replied.

Mr. Grimes was very angry. He looked at Jim and said, "What in the hell is going on in this zoo? Where are our damned parts?"

Jim said, "I'll go check with Buck." Mr. Grimes accompanied him to the loading dock.

As soon as they left, the group around Tony's cell broke up. Gus and Frank walked back to the tool crib, arguing all the way about the boring bar. I went back to my machine and started to tear down the wasted setup. I figured it was better to just keep my head down and start the next job.

Talk about waste! Maybe I'll have some time to figure out how much time was wasted in this fire drill. Tony and his mill operator just stood around their ACME 1000 with nothing to do. They were nervous because they both knew that Mr. Grimes would be back to see them.

Jim and Mr. Grimes arrived at the loading dock. They asked Buck where the stuff from the plater was. Buck pointed to the three pallets sitting over in the receiving area. Mr. Grimes said, "We're supposed to have a pallet of pump bodies. Those pallets have valve bodies. That rush order of pumps has to go out today!" Buck told Mr. Grimes that the pallets of valve bodies were all that the plater had dropped off that morning.

Mr. Grimes said to Jim, "I'm going back to my office. Find out where those pump bodies are and let me know!" He turned and walked toward his office. Jim went to the phone on the receiving desk and called the plater.

"Sullivan's Plating, Sully speaking."

Jim said, "Hi Sully, this is Jim over at Quality Pump. We were supposed to have some pump bodies galvanized and have them back today."

Sully said, "Well, you ain't getting them today. They're right here in front of me."

Jim exclaimed, "Sully, we've got to have those parts today!"

"Hey," Sully replied. "You guys will never learn, will you? I don't know how many times we've told you, if you want your order the next day, you have to have it here by 10:00 A.M. That's 10:00 A.M. in our facility, not on your dock.

"I don't want to teach you guys arithmetic, but it takes fifteen minutes to get here from your dock. Your guy has to allow fifteen minutes for traffic holdups. Now, I figure your guy has to leave your dock at 9:30 A.M. That seems pretty simple, doesn't it?

"Your truck pulled in here at 11:30 A.M. yesterday, and by that time all the racks were filled on the plater and we were putting them in the bath."

"OK" Jim said, "when's the soonest we can get them back?"

Sully replied, "If you want to pay the overtime, I can have a guy stay late tonight. He can wash 'em off and load them on a pallet. You can pick them up at 7 A.M., when we open."

Jim said "OK, do that and I'll have a truck there in the morning when you open."

Jim got off the phone and went over to Buck. He told him to have a truck at Sullivan's at 7 A.M. and then asked him why the truck was late to the plater's. Buck told him that he had held the truck for those specific parts, and that they had left as soon as they could.

Jim said, "OK, I understand, Buck. This is going to be a good problem to deal with in class tomorrow."

Dr. Elbie and Jim were already in the classroom when I arrived for class the next morning. They were standing by the desk huddled in deep conversation.

Gus and his crew came in. Gus was still bitching about the boring bar from yesterday's setup.

Everybody in class was talking about what had happened the day before. Normally, we wouldn't have talked about an incident like this in front of the managers. Today, it seemed OK.

Dr. Elbie finished talking with Jim, went to the board and wrote *single point of control*. He turned to the class and said, "I understand we had a little Keystone Cops routine here yesterday." Everyone in the class started talking at once. Gus and Frank were still going at each other about the boring bar. Tony was saying that it wasn't his fault, that the order came from "on high." Bernard was telling everyone who would listen that this kind of stuff happens all the time.

Dr. Elbie raised his hand and yelled, "Hold it!" The class quieted down.

He continued, "Remember: No Blame! There's a lot of information on waste we can capture from yesterday's events, but only if we go about it in a structured, scientific way."

The door opened and Mr. Grimes entered. He sat down and Dr. Elbie continued, "OK, as I was saying, we can learn a lot from yesterday, but we have to approach it as we would any other problem. I can tell you from past experience that situations like what led to yesterday's screw-up are not just on the shop floor, they're throughout the company. Solving these problems is going to have far-reaching consequences throughout the company.

"I know everyone is hot to put out this fire, but it's just like fighting a real fire. You have to bring the proper equipment to the event. So, step-by-step, let's look at the wastes involved, how much they cost, the causes of the wastes and any possible solutions."

After Dr. Elbie spoke everyone calmed down and started to analyze the waste. We talked about the importance of a single point of control. Everyone could see that was the real cause of the recent problem. But it wasn't the only cause. It was just the trigger that set off a series of problems.

For the rest of the class that day, and for the next two sessions, we worked on wastes that we found arising out of this one situation. We had lists of problems and solutions. Dr. Elbie had been right. The causes of this problem *were* spread throughout the company. At the end of class on Friday, Dr. Elbie said, "OK, we've addressed the problems within the company, but there's one very important detail that we have overlooked. Where were the pump bodies that were to be machined? Think about that over the weekend."

10

I got to work a little early on Monday morning. The classroom was open, so I went in to finish my coffee. Buck was already in the room. He was looking at the bulletin board and smiling again. When I walked over and joined him, I saw that Mr. Grimes had placed another memo on the board. It had been put over the one from the week before and said in big red letters:

#1 Priority:
A Single Point of Control!!!

Buck said, "Man, look at this. What'd I tell you?" Buck took the old memo off the board and stuck it in his pocket. The classroom started to fill up so I went back to my seat. Jim, Mr. Grimes and Ed Daley came in and sat down.

Dr. Elbie entered the classroom. As he put his books and paperwork on the desk, he asked, "Did anyone figure out where the pump bodies were?"

There was a general groan from the class. Dr. Elbie smiled, and said, "Did anybody here see *Stand and Deliver?*" A few hands went up.

"You know, the movie about Jaime Escalante, the high school teacher in Los Angeles who taught Latino teenagers calculus. In the movie he tells his students, 'This is easy! You already know how to do it. You go step-by-step.' And that, my friends, is exactly how we are going to do it: step-by-step."

When Dr. Elbie said that, I suddenly felt better about being in the class. Over the weekend, I had thought about where the pump bodies were and how they got there. Sandy had commented to me that when I worked at Osgood's, I had weekends off. Now, she said, I was thinking about Quality Pump all the time. I was spending my weekends doing work. She didn't have a problem with that. She was just worried about going through another plant closure. One in a lifetime was enough.

Although I thought about pump bodies all weekend, I was not able to come up with any solutions. I figured maybe I didn't know what I was doing yet and needed better tools.

Buck raised his hand, "They were at the plater. The pump bodies were at the plater."

Dr. Elbie asked Buck why they hadn't returned here as scheduled. Buck started to reply when he was interrupted by Jim.

Jim said, "The problem isn't with the plater, it's with us. I asked Ed Daley to come by today because we're going to have to discuss some changes in the work rules to solve this problem. I wanted him to be here to advise us during these discussions. The problem is pretty straightforward and I hope we can come up with an easy solution."

Jim sent someone out to fetch Mike Cain. Mike was in charge of quality control and was the key guy who checks all parts before they go to the plater.

As soon as Mike came in and sat down, Jim continued, "In order for us to get next-day service from the plater, we have to have our material at the plater's by 10:00 A.M. The problem lies in the quality inspection before they are trucked to the plater. Last week when this came up, I was ready to blame Buck, but it's not his fault. The inspection has to be done before they're released to the loading dock for shipping.

"Unfortunately, Mike Cain has many duties besides inspection. What I propose is that Mike and a helper come in an hour early to get the inspection done before the plant opens. Over the weekend, I talked this over with Dr. Elbie. We both know that it's just a stopgap measure but we have an immediate problem and we need to deal with it now.

"Hopefully, we can find the real cause of the delays and can come up with a permanent solution to this problem soon. We need a solution that will get Mike and his helper back to their regular shifts. I have asked Ed to talk about the work rules and how your contract reads. We would appreciate any input you could give us."

Mike Cain stood up and said, "What the hell is going on here? I don't want to come in an hour early because you guys can't get the work out on time! This is bullshit!"

Jim replied, "Mike, this is only a stopgap measure for a few weeks, a couple of months at the most. We need to do this until we can get you some help to do the inspection."

Mike and Mr. Grimes knew each other a long time. Mike started at Quality Pump when the plant was still downtown. Mr. Grimes got him into the machinists' union and he served his apprenticeship at Quality Pump and had been employed there ever since.

Mike appealed directly to Mr. Grimes. "John," he said, "I don't want to do this. There must be another way to get this resolved. Get someone else to come in early."

Mr. Grimes remained seated, although he turned in his chair to face Mike. He said, "Mike, we go back a long way. Everyone in this organization is making some kind of sacrifice to make this change process work. I'm asking you to do this for the company and as a personal favor to me."

Mike grudgingly agreed and said, "I'll do it for a little while, but I'm concerned over the work rule changes. Once the rule is changed, what's to keep it from becoming permanent? If this starts, when is it going to stop?" There was a general murmur of agreement from the class.

Ed Daley walked to the front of the class. "Most of you know me, but for those of you who don't, my name is Ed Daley and I'm the business agent for your machinists' local. When Jim called me the other day to talk about the work rules, I knew that there would be some opposition to the changes. I've seen the effects of this training on several local companies that have collective bargaining agreements, and I must say that after the training was completed, those companies were a better place to work for everyone.

"Many of you are aware that manufacturers with union agreements face stiff competition from not only foreign competitors, but also from other U.S. companies that either manufacture in open shops, or have their plants outside the United States. You're all aware that a few months ago Osgood Manufacturing closed its plant here and shipped its equipment to Mexico.

"Many of the people who worked at Osgood's are no longer working as machinists. They're working at K-Mart selling tools or at McDonald's flipping hamburgers. They're not making near the money that you are, and forget about any health or retirement benefits.

"Some of you here worked at Osgood's and I know you had a difficult time finding other work that paid a decent wage. The point of all this is that Quality Pump is willing to make an investment to make this plant work.

"Having Dr. Elbie and his group come in to train you is very expensive for Mr. Grimes. Remember, you people are still being paid while you're attending this class. Mr. Grimes is paying for other classes as well. He pays for us to attend work-related classes at the community college and he is also paying the fees for the literacy and English as a

The New Turnaround

second language (ESL) programs at the community college, for those of you who need it.

"As your president, I must tell you that union workers are in a fight for their lives. I don't think a few minor changes in the work rules is anything to bitch about. I'm willing to work with Mr. Grimes and Dr. Elbie on your behalf, but you people will have to cooperate to insure that these changes will work and that this company stays in business."

Ed asked if there were any questions. He was pretty good. Everything he said was true. I think most of the people in the class realized it.

As Ed walked toward the door, Mr. Grimes, Mike and Jim followed him. Outside they shook hands and Jim and Mr. Grimes returned to the classroom.

Dr. Elbie said, "OK, now you all know. Mr. Daley let the cat out of the bag. I do charge for my services.

"I appreciate what Ed had to say. I hope you all realize that if you're asked to do something different, either by us or by your team members, you're not being singled out. And these changes are not a punishment. All of you will be asked to make some sacrifices while the changes are taking place.

"Before we get too far into this problem, I would like to take a few minutes to review a technique that I have used in the past to handle this type of situation with the truck and the plater. It can be used for other problems, but let's again apply it to the truck and its schedule. Remember the Yes/No Charts?

"Let me explain. Buck, what time is the truck supposed to leave?"

Buck was paying attention and immediately responded, "9:30 A.M., sir!"

"OK. Why is it supposed to leave at 9:30 A.M.?"

"Because Sully and other people on the truck's delivery route expect us to be there at certain times and 9:30 A.M. is the right time for the truck to leave," Buck responded.

"So all these other people are dependent upon the truck leaving at 9:30 A.M. on the button. Does it ever do so?" Dr. Elbie smiled with his question.

"Almost never," was Buck's reply. "We try but we never can."

"OK, here is where the Yes/No Chart comes in. If something is important, then measure it. Put a chart up on the wall. Put a mark on the chart when the truck leaves late on a particular day. That's the way we can measure the truck's performance. So, what is the goal of Buck's loading dock crew?"

Andrew, the engineer, said, "We want to measure whether the truck leaves by 9:30 A.M. every day. *No excuses and no blame.* Just, did it leave on time. I think that's what you are getting at, right?"

"You've got that right. Does everyone follow what we are doing here?" Dr. Elbie was serious as he scanned the class. "Good, now all we have to do is get Buck to put the Yes/No Chart up in his department.

"Let's see what other examples we can find. After we do, let's create a Yes/No Chart and start keeping records," Dr. Elbie continued.

Jim put his hand up. "You know, we expedite an awful lot of orders through the plant and each order forces us to change the schedule. When we change the schedule, we pay lots of money in overtime. So I want to set up a Yes/No Chart to determine how many days we have expedites. I know it's a lot, but if we record it and post it for everyone to see, maybe we can bring that under control. I'll start today."

Dr. Elbie smiled. "See how easy it is? Once you get a feel for it, you'll find that out. Do we have any ideas for other important things to measure?"

Hands immediately shot up with the following possibilities:

"Do we have a new schedule defined for the truck? (yes/no)"
"Do we have boxes to put the parts in? (yes/no)"
"Were materials ready when setups were complete? (yes/no)"
"Were all the proper tools ready when the job was started in the shop? (yes/no)"
(When the answers to these questions are yes, they are no longer problems.)

The list grew quickly with everyone contributing great ideas. Before long, Dr. Elbie said, "I guess you people understand this. The most important part of the process is to collect the data on a No Blame basis. Either the answer is yes or it is no. There are no gray areas."

Buck was bothered by this. "You mean to tell me if the truck leaves at 9:31 A.M. that I check NO? That's pretty hard. There are always reasons for being a few minutes late."

Dr. Elbie responded, "I know, and that's why we have problems. There are always good excuses. The corollary to No Blame is

The New Turnaround

"In other words, Buck, you set up a rule and then you measure it with No Blame. Report the facts. If it is unreasonable for the truck to leave at 9:30 A.M. then change the time. You have a goal of making sure that the truck leaves every day at 9:30 A.M., not 9:31 A.M. That's pretty simple. Once you understand that, then when the truck leaves late for four or five days you will know what to do. You set up a process to monitor the situation when the truck fails to leave on time and then proceed.

"Does everyone understand this?"

Gus said, "This is really chicken. I don't want to measure something when I know the answer is always going to be NO. Doesn't this get people mad?"

"Yes, it does," said Dr. Elbie, "and you know what? People hate to see lots of nos on the chart. And you know what happens?"

Buck chimed in, "I know what I would do, I'd fix the son of a bitch. That's what I'd do!"

"And you know Buck, that's what everyone else does. No one wants to leave those problems glaring at them. So they organize their teams to fix them. Why don't you set up Yes/No Charts for the items that we discussed and I'll be by this afternoon to look at them. It's easy; don't make it hard."

Tony raised his hand and said, "Dr. Elbie, we've spent a lot of time talking about teams and we've broken up the class into teams to analyze waste and stuff. I don't have any idea, outside of the crew I work with, which team I'm on."

"Thank you very much, Tony. That's exactly what we're going to talk about next—teams. I don't know what team you're supposed to be on either. You're the ones who are doing the work. Ask yourselves: What work is being done by this team?

"Remember when I talked about a business being no different than a baseball team, and that there were teams within teams?

"You've had a couple of weeks to see the problems in this company and to think about solutions. One of the first problems you are going to have to confront is who's on a specific team. Some of you will be on just one team, some of you will be on several.

"I know from experience generally how the teams are going to form, but I am not going to assign you to a team.

"My job is to be a facilitator. I am not here to assign jobs. I am here to make you stretch to find your own solutions. I will tell you that some of the teams you form will not be in existence in a couple of months. At least not in their original form.

"Some of you will naturally be team players and some of you won't. The ones who are hesitant to participate in the team process are going to have real problems here.

"The thing about change is that you're always taking a chance when you try something new. Here you're not penalized for failure, you're encouraged to try again. Remember, *NO BLAME!*"

After class was over we went to the shop floor and discussed teams. We broke up into small groups, mostly along the lines of what we did in the plant. The CNC people together, the quality people, the setup crew, and the rest. In my group, there was Billy and Tony, the two lead men for the ACME milling machines, myself and a couple of other mill operators. A guy named Glenn who worked on another kind of milling machine, an XS 2040, had nobody to team up with so we invited him to join our group.

We all decided that Billy's cell would be one team and that Tony would have another, but we would also be a team together. We talked it over among ourselves and decided to approach Gus about having a person from the setup crew be a part of both teams. Billy went over and talked to Gus and Gus said it was all right with him, if somebody would volunteer. Frank was still getting some grief from Gus about the boring bar incident so he was happy to come and join our group.

We decided to try a completely new setup. We had a new industrial pump that just came out of Research & Development and we were about to put it into production. It made sense to start fresh with a new product and to see how this team stuff would affect the overall manufacturing process, rather than try to take existing processes and change them around.

We were pretty excited about this idea and Tony asked if we'd stay after work for a while to kick it around. We all agreed that we would stay to go over the project.

I called Sandy at lunch and told her that I would be a little late getting home for dinner. She said that it was OK, but, nevertheless, she was concerned that I was working late. It was hard to explain but it was different than in earlier times. In those cases, it was just work. In this case it was working with others to improve our business. That was different.

Billy and I punched out at the end of the day and went over to meet the rest of the group in the classroom. Tony came in with a couple of six packs of soda. Ever since one of the companies in town was sued for serving beer on the premises to an employee who was later in a serious car accident, none of the companies allowed any drinking on their premises. Mr. Grimes hated to have that rule but he had no choice.

Tony had the plans for the new pump tucked under his arm, and he tacked them on a portable easel.

He stepped back from the easel, popped open a soda can and said, "Boy, this sure is a mess!"

He was right. The piece that we had to make was going to be milled out of a solid block of aluminum. It was an integral part of a control system that was going to be the central component of a computer-controlled heating and air conditioning system. It wasn't really square, but then again it wasn't really round either. It had a semicircular distribution turret cut into one end that housed five or six small valves. All in all, it was a complicated process to take this from a hunk of metal to a finished assembly.

We all had our chairs arranged in a semicircle in front of the easel. Tony sat down and looked at the drawing. "Does anyone have a clue how we're going to make this?" he asked.

Billy went up to the easel and started measuring the drawing to see how much material needed to be taken out of the block just to shape it to the outside dimensions.

Jim walked by the classroom and came in. "What's all this?" he said. "I thought you would be gone by now."

Billy explained what we were doing. Then he asked, "Jim, how many of these are we going to build? These things are complicated and they're going to be difficult to machine. Just to get the rough cut size is going to take forever."

Jim replied, "From what I gather, this is going to be a very big item for us. Several large air conditioning manufacturers have already expressed interest in the pump and its control system. So I think in the next couple of years it's going to account for a large portion of our business. It depends, of course, on whether or not we can manufacture it competitively."

His statement put things in perspective. This was an important item not only for the company but for our future as well.

The workers from both ACME cells were in the meeting, as well as Frank, the setup guy, and Glenn, our lone XS 2040 operator.

We kicked it around for a while. We were wondering how we were going to remove all the material. Glenn finally said, "Look, the ACME 1000 is a fine little machine, but let me take a run at the major cutting with my machine. I don't have the tool capacity of your machines. I'll get the parts roughed out on my XS using the big cutters and hog out a lot of material in one pass. You guys say that it will take over three minutes to do the first cut for this body. An XS machine can do it in less than forty seconds, maybe even thirty. If I cut the bodies just a little oversize, then you can finish them up on your machines."

What he said seemed like a good solution on the face of it, but it didn't really work. The XSs and ACMEs were in two totally separate cells in different areas of the company. There were different programmers assigned to each of the machines and we just didn't see how we could connect the two. We spent a while trying to figure out if it was possible to follow up on Glenn's suggestion.

Then I looked up at the clock and saw that it was 6:30. I jumped up and exclaimed, "Holy cow! I gotta get out of here. I told my wife that I would be home for dinner and that was a half-hour ago!" As I ran for the door the meeting started to break up.

As soon as I arrived home, Cathy, my little girl, ran up to me. "Daddy, Daddy, where were you? Mommy said you would be here for dinner. We waited and waited but you never came. We had to eat by ourselves," she said.

Sandy walked into the living room. She had just put Mickey to bed. She said, "Cathy, go get ready for bed. After you've brushed your teeth I'll come in and read you a story."

Cathy protested that she hadn't been able to see me and that it wasn't fair that she had to go to bed so soon. Her mom said, "None of that, now you go get ready and we'll both be there in a few minutes."

I was sitting on the couch when Sandy came and stood over me. She rested her hand on the arm of the couch and with her other hand wagged a finger in my face. "I'd better not find any lipstick on your collar!"

"Your dinner's in the oven. When you're finished, would you come

The New Turnaround

in for a minute? Cathy got a little upset tonight because she isn't used to you not being here for dinner."

I went into the kitchen and leaned against the counter. I was pretty tired.

Buddy came in the back door. I gave him a hug and he went off to his room to do some math homework and work on a project for his art class.

I finished my dinner and put the plate in with the rest of the dirty dishes.

As I closed the refrigerator door, Sandy walked in and said, "Don't drink out of the milk carton! Cathy and Buddy have seen you do it and now they're starting to do it!" After the scolding, I put the milk away.

As Sandy started on the dishes, I went in to say goodnight to my little girl. When I got back to the kitchen, I picked up a towel and dried the dishes.

Sandy asked, "What's going on at the plant? You've never been late getting home before. Is everything all right?"

We spent a long time talking in the kitchen, as we cleaned up. I told her about going to class and about how things were changing at work. I said, "It's exciting, but at the same time it's scary. If this doesn't work out, there is a good possibility that Quality could close down."

Sandy replied, "I know you're a smart guy. If anyone can figure this thing out, it's you. Your dad says that you're one of the best machinists he's ever known. It sounds like the people you work with are pretty smart too. I think all of this will work out OK."

We sat at the kitchen table and I told her about all the hassles with the manufacturing of this new product line. I told her about Glenn's solution and how much fun it was to participate in this kind of work. It was good to hear Glenn give some input.

The only problem with Glenn's solution was the waste that it created in moving the product from one operating area to another. How could we get good production out of two different cells with different machines without spending all of our time moving WIP around the shop?

"Why can't you just move that XS machine over next to yours?" Sandy asked.

I explained that they used different programs and programmers and that this was just one job. She replied, "But honey, if this is going to account for so much of the company's income, shouldn't you try to build it in the most efficient way?" My God, she sounded just like Dr. Elbie.

She went on, "Even if that XS thing sits idle every once and a while, wouldn't that be cheaper than moving all those parts around? I mean, how much could that machine be worth?" When I told her three hundred thousand dollars, she let out a low whistle, and said, "OK, I'll shut up now."

It was late when we finally got to bed. I lay awake with Sandy's comments running through my head. I thought, why couldn't we move one of the XSs over to our cell?

11

Glenn was in the classroom the next morning when I arrived. He had his nose in a programming book. He looked up from the book and asked me if I had any experience with programming. I told him that I did and he said, "I've been looking at this programming book and although I don't understand it very well, it seems to me that we could take one of those XS machines and move it into an ACME cell without too much trouble."

I looked at the programming book and I'll be damned if he wasn't right. We could run both machines off one computer with only minor reprogramming!

I said, "Glenn, this is funny because my wife suggested the same thing last night. We'd have to check it out with the programmers, but from what this book says, I think you're right. We *could* move an XS into our cell."

Billy walked in with Gus and joined us. I showed them the book. "Hey, Billy," I said. "Glenn figures that we could move one of his machines to our cell. It sure would eliminate a lot of waste created by moving stuff around. What do you think?"

Billy replied, "I had the same thought last night. Tony and I stuck around for a while after you left. He's talking to Jim right now to see if we can get the projected sales figures. If we're going to build enough of these things, it makes a lot of sense."

Bernard overheard our conversation as he walked by. "What're you guys trying to do?" he asked. "Move an XS machine in with the AC-MEs? Man, that would never work! Just the logistics of walking back and forth from programming to the cell would take up a good portion of the day."

Billy replied, "According to this programming book, it can be done, and fairly easily. And by the way, Bernard, why are you programmers so far away from the machines? Every time we have to make an adjustment we have to walk halfway to China. I think we ought to propose moving the programmers out onto the shop floor. It sure would save a lot of time."

Bernard took a step back. It was like someone had hit him with an overhand right. "That's crazy!" he exclaimed. "We aren't machinists.

We're programmers. Those computers wouldn't survive on the shop floor!"

Bernard was kind of snooty and he didn't like the thought of being out on the shop floor with all the riff-raff. I had a hunch that it wasn't the computers that Bernard was worried about, it was the programmers.

It was a few minutes after seven when Dr. Elbie came in and called the class to attention. "I know I'm a few minutes late and I apologize. Waste is waste. Just because I was 6 minutes late, I caused 144 minutes of waste. If you add up all the minutes that people were waiting, it totals 144 minutes, or 6 minutes times 24 people. You see the impact, don't you? Since this is the only class that I am likely to be late for, I'm going to make you a deal. I'm going to spot you another 1,000 minutes, so you'll have 1,144 minutes. I'm going to make you a bet that by the time these classes are over the whole organization can't reduce aggregate setup time each week by more than those 1,144 minutes.

"We will define the aggregate setup like this: We'll add up the total setup for all the CNC machines each week. We'll average the last four weeks. If you can cut 1,144 minutes off that weekly total, you win. If you don't, I win. The loser buys pizza and beer for everyone in the company."

At that point Andrew said, "I don't think that's a very fair bet. You know that we can't do it. That's why you made it."

Dr. Elbie smiled and responded, "Andrew, I'm ashamed of you. You just insulted everyone in the company. You called them lily-livered, yellow-bellied snakes. You implied that they weren't up to the challenge. Does anyone agree with Andrew?"

Tony jumped right in with both feet. "Hey, Andrew was just trying to protect us, weren't you?" And he looked at Andrew. Andrew smiled and nodded.

Tony went on, "I like that bet. Hell, if we lose, we'll have to buy about fifteen pizzas and some beer. That's only ten dollars per person. Now if we win, it's going to cost our fine leader up there over $200. I'm all for the bet and I think we will win. If you want my ten cents, let's do it!"

Everyone agreed unanimously that we were up to the challenge and that we would win easily. We didn't quite know how but we felt confident that we would figure it out.

Dr. Elbie had taken off his coat and had on a T-shirt with a picture of Einstein and a quote underneath that said:

> **Imagination is more
> important than knowledge.**
> **—Einstein**

Dr. Elbie began, "OK, now we're going to chip away at the setup minutes that I bet you. Remember, here you are not rewarded for keeping secrets. The only way your jobs are going to get better is if you share ideas. So who wants to start?"

Bernard raised his hand, and said, "The ACME team is going crazy. They think that they can move an XS into the same cell and run it off the same computer. They even think that the programmers should move out onto the shop floor!"

"Why is that such a crazy idea?" Dr. Elbie asked.

Bernard testily replied, "Because we're programmers! We work in an office!"

Dr. Elbie just looked at him and asked, "Why?"

Bernard got real shrill. He sounded like Don Knotts. "Because we're programmers!"

Dr. Elbie said, "Why, again? That is not an acceptable answer. Why not! I think that moving the programmers to the shop floor merits some investigation. Does anyone else have any ideas on this subject?"

Tony said, "Last night Billy and I measured the time that it takes to go from the ACME 1000 cells to the programming office. We walked at a normal pace. One way is about one minute and forty seconds. We figure that on the average setup we have face-to-face communication at the computer or at the machine three times. That's almost ten minutes wasted on every setup. And that doesn't include the waiting time for the inspector, setup man, operator or the machine."

Mr. Grimes got up and walked to the front of the room. "OK, let's think about this for a minute. I'm intrigued by this idea. Let's say, for the sake of argument, that you and two other people have to wait while these other people walk back and forth to do programming. My God, that's half an hour each time you set up. Tony, how many setups do you average a week?"

Tony replied, "Oh, probably between thirty-five and forty for the whole shop."

Mr. Grimes said, "OK, Tony, help me on this. To be conservative, we'll say thirty setups per week. That's fifteen hours of wasted time each week, thirty minutes of waste on each setup. You take that number times our figure of $25 an hour, that's $375 a week, or $18,750 per year. Walking can add up pretty damn quickly!"

Jim was taking notes. You could just see the look of disbelief on his face.

Dr. Elbie laughed and said, "Isn't it amazing how simple things can add up to big bucks? It appears to me that we can all agree that moving the programmers out to the shop should be investigated. Oh, by the way, that's 900 minutes, (thirty setups at thirty minutes apiece) that got knocked off your handicap."

He had bet us that we would not reduce 1144 minutes off the setup. In this example alone we would take 900 minutes out of the loop by just moving the programmers out to the shop. By my calculations, we only had 244 minutes to go. It was starting to look very easy.

Dr. Elbie continued, "Now, the other issue that was raised is, should one of the XS machines be moved into an ACME cell to produce this one product? Bonnie, do you have any sales projections that we could use to justify our decisions?"

Bonnie huddled with her boss, Roland, for a minute or two. Finally, she said, "We don't have any firm sales projections at this moment. We have signed one order with a major heating and air conditioning manufacturer. We're now negotiating with two others. Both Roland and I think that this pump and valve assembly is going to be a big seller. It eliminates the need for a separate control valve for each pump. I'll have some projected sales figures for you in the morning."

Everybody was getting ready to leave and Dr. Elbie said, "Wait just a minute! Class isn't over yet. I have one thing to go over with you before you leave. Did you know that you learned something today that I was going to teach you tomorrow? I was going to teach the Five Why's. Does anyone know about the Five Why's?"

No one responded. Dr. Elbie went on, "Taiichi Ohno, the Japanese developer of the Toyota production system, said that the answer to all problems can be determined by the time you come up with the fifth why. You might recall that I interrogated Bernard about why he shouldn't move to the shop floor. By the second why, we realized that Bernard did not have a good reason and that we should investigate it further.

"The same thing applies to any other problem. For example, Jim was telling me about a problem he had with someone who tripped over a hose and got hurt. He asked the *first why*. The answer was that one of the workers was using the air hose to blow off a machine. The *second why* revealed that the worker using the hose didn't have a hose on his side of the aisle. *Third why*, because there was no air line near his work area. The answer is, why not put an air line near his work area? The answer was obtained by the third why.

"So your homework assignment is to practice the Five Why's today and forever. Remember, this is just like a two-year-old asking you why. Whenever I've worked with people and they know the Five Why's, I never have to ask the second why. They know the next one is coming and so they try to come up with a solution quickly. Most people hate to hear the second why. Have a good day, everyone!"

12

The next morning Dr. Elbie was waiting for us when we arrived for class. Standing with him near the desk was another man. He was short and wore his hair back in a ponytail. He was dressed in blue jeans, an open-necked sports shirt, a sports coat and cowboy boots. I thought to myself, "What is this hippie going to teach us?" As soon as the class settled down, Dr. Elbie said, "This is Phil, and he's going to teach you about a technique that you should know if you want to win my bet with you. It is called SMED."

Dr. Elbie turned the meeting over to Phil. He introduced himself to us, "Thanks, Jack. My name is Phil and I'm here to talk to you about SMED." As he spoke, he walked over to the board and wrote SINGLE MINUTE EXCHANGE of DIES.

"Single minute exchange of dies is a philosophy of manufacturing that differs radically from anything used in America since the Industrial Revolution," he explained. "It not only addresses the issue of setup, but it also looks at the whole idea of batch sizes, economic order, quantity and many other interesting areas. For instance, if we reduce setup time to ten minutes on any of your current jobs, what other problems does that create?"

Buck was really interested in what Phil was saying. He raised his hand. "Phil, I think that it would be a miracle if you could get a setup done in this place in less than ten minutes. That seems almost impossible, although I don't know much about machining. Why would you even suggest such a ridiculous thing?"

Phil responded, "Is what I suggested ridiculous?"

Tony said, "I have no idea where you are going to take this discussion, but did I hear you right, a ten minute setup?"

Phil went to the front of the room and pulled himself up on the table. "Yes, I did say ten minutes! Right now you may think this is a crazy notion, but it works. It really does! Over the next several days we're going to go over many examples to make this idea clearer for you."

Phil looked at Tony and asked his name. Tony responded, and Phil continued. "Tony, you will be surprised at how simple this is. It is truly a great idea.

"As you have been hearing in class for the last couple of weeks, we are great believers in low-tech solutions. To us, a low-tech solution requires a small investment in equipment or resources to solve a problem. These low-tech solutions usually create a major change in your system of doing things. They usually don't require any new equipment, merely the better utilization of equipment you currently have.

"The idea of SMED was contributed by a Japanese manufacturing engineer, Shigeo Shingo. He initially applied this concept to the changeover of dies in an automobile plant, but it applies equally well to a machine shop operation. As we'll discuss later, it applies to a clerk processing paperwork in the front office as well.

"The Japanese have been proponents of this philosophy for years. They have been able to take a nine hour setup down to nine minutes! All of this without new machines or major capital outlay.

"SMED involves three very simple steps: First, you separate the internal and the external setups. We'll explain this momentarily; then you simplify, and finally you optimize. The rules of SMED are: 1. separate 2. simplify 3. optimize.

"Before getting heavily into this, let me give you a little bit of my background. I have a basic high school education. I served an apprenticeship in a machine shop for several years. For a number of reasons, mostly economic, I started looking around for something else to do.

"I had known Jack Elbie socially for quite a while. He asked me to go to work for him as an instructor, in spite of, or maybe because of, my somewhat limited formal education. I've been working for Jack for a couple of years, kind of like the sorcerer's apprentice.

"The point of all this is, you don't have to be a rocket scientist to figure this stuff out. There is nothing that is going to be taught in any of these classes that you cannot master.

"Jack and I have prepared a work sheet on one setup from this factory. It was taken from a setup in this plant and is a good example of what can be achieved. Here is what was found."

25 minutes to tear down the last job
30 minutes to clean the machine
80 minutes to find the tools and talk with the tool crib manager
80 minutes to set the tool offsets in the holders
15 minutes to find the programmer to load the program

15 minutes to download the program while waiting for the programmer to find the current version of the program to download

30 minutes to find that the program had two bugs in it and then make the corrections

25 minutes to load all the tools

25 minutes to get the first article through all four vise operations

20 minutes to find the inspector for the first article

30 minutes for first article inspection

15 minutes to correct the program and

30 minutes for another first article.

"The final inspection was another 30 minutes because the inspector stayed at the station and waited for the part. In all, it took you 450 minutes to do this particular changeover. 420 minutes plus the extra 30 minutes. I think that you said," and he pointed to me, "it was close to 7 hours. According to my calculations, it was exactly 7½ hours."

"When you look back at that job, how much of the time could have been spent in preparation before the previous job stopped? We call that time external setup time. In other words, *external setup* is work that can be done while another job is running. *Internal setup* is setup work that can only be done when the machine is stopped. In analyzing this job, how many of those operations can be moved to external setup? This is what is known as the separation phase of SMED. It is the first step."

Tony said, "You can't tear down the previous job before the machine stops. So the first step there is internal setup. Is that right?"

Phil nodded and encouraged Tony. "I think you've got it, keep going!"

Tony said, "Cleaning the machines is clearly internal."

Bonnie jumped in ahead of Tony and said, "Finding tools has got to be an external setup issue."

Tony took over again, "And measuring tool offsets is an internal function because it can only be done while the spindle . . . No, I see. It can be an external setup because we can do it while the spindle is turning on the previous job. We may have to buy a few more tools but it would be a minor expense to move that operation to external setup."

At that point Bernard said, "Finding me has got to be an internal setup because I can't waste my time waiting for the machine to stop. It would be very inefficient to have me waiting while the machine was still cutting parts."

Phil smiled at Bernard and asked the usual question. "Bernard, do you add value to the process?"

Bernard was almost offended by the question but Buck jumped right in. "Bernard is no different than me. He doesn't add value. He is necessary support but he doesn't add value. Why'd you ask that question?"

Phil smiled in Buck's direction and asked, "And you're Buck, am I right?" Buck acknowledged as much.

Phil continued, "Our goal is to design a factory so that the people who add value can keep doing so. When we say that we want them adding value, it means the same as making money for the company. The machinists and assemblers are the only people who can add value. Is that right?"

Mr. Grimes had been sitting quietly while Phil had introduced himself and carried on the class. Out of nowhere, he said, "I see what you're saying. Yeah, now it makes sense." Mr. Grimes was mumbling to himself. "Yeah, I really see it," he said.

Everybody suddenly was looking around the room and then began to get worried. It looked like Mr. Grimes had flipped out.

Suddenly Mr. Grimes stood up and faced the class. "I'm sorry for blurting that out in class and out of turn, but I suddenly saw what Dr. Elbie was talking about." He looked at me and asked, "Remember when he came out to the shop with Jim and explained the concept of profitability to me?"

I nodded that I remembered. I remembered the discussion but I didn't understand anything that was said.

"Dr. Elbie was right. If we really want to make this company profitable, let's make setup zero! Damnit, we can get close. I see it now. It makes sense. Does everybody else see that?

"I have to admit it. I didn't understand until now. Phil, you did a wonderful thing! You made me see the light. I'm sorry, let's keep going here."

Phil said, "I get excited when someone can see what's going on. Thank you very much, Mr. Grimes. Maybe as we proceed we can even make a believer out of Tony."

Tony stood up and joked, "I believe, Phil! I believe!"

Phil continued, "With my conversion record we ought to go into the religion business! Anyway, let's continue." Phil went to the overhead projector and showed us the following breakdown of the setup:

External Setup		Internal Setup	
		25 minutes	Tear down
		30 minutes	Clean Machine
80 minutes	Find tools		
80 minutes	Set tool offsets		
15 minutes	Find programmer		
		15 minutes	Load program
		30 minutes	Correct program and adjust
		25 minutes	Load tools
		25 minutes	First article
20 minutes	Find inspector		
		30 minutes	First article inspection
		15 minutes	Program correction
		30 minutes	Machine first article again
		30 minutes	First article inspection
			START JOB
195 MINUTES = TOTAL		255 MINUTES = TOTAL	

"So in all, there is a potential savings of over three hours in the machine stoppage just by planning your work differently. We call this the separation part of SMED, because you first separate internal from external setup.

"As a way of illustrating, let's look at programmer time in this process. If you let the programmers know you have a job closing down in the next hour, they can plan their work to accommodate you. You can reduce your setup time to a little over four hours. That is a 43% reduction in the setup time by just planning your work more intelligently. Do you see what I mean?

"It looks to me like you guys can take the bet from Dr. Elbie with no problem. Any comments?"

The New Turnaround

Tony said, "That's really amazing! We can save that time! I can't believe it! Why have we been so stupid?"

Mr. Grimes stood up again. "Tony, you people aren't stupid. If anyone was stupid it was me, because I established a system that didn't allow you to have any input. Even if you had come up with the idea of using SMED, we wouldn't have allowed your input." Mr. Grimes looked at me. "I really thank you for collecting this information for us. Thanks again. I see how we can fix this place. It's starting to make sense."

As I looked at the overhead, I was also amazed. When I looked at the process like this, I really saw how we could make some improvements.

When Dr. Elbie asked me some time ago whether I could improve my performance, I never thought it might come to this. It was so simple. We could easily reduce setup time by over half. It would take only a few easy changes in the way we did things.

Phil went on, "You can see from the sheet that we haven't eliminated any steps. We have, however, greatly reduced the setup time by simply dividing the work into two groups. *Internal setup,* that which can only be done when the machine is stopped, and *external setup,* anything that can be done outside the machine while it is still running.

"This is a pretty simple process. In the days of cheap labor and relatively inexpensive machinery, setup was not as critical to plant survival as it is today. Now it can really make the difference between a company making or losing money. It isn't going to solve all your problems but it lets you breathe a little while you try.

"As you drive setup time down, a whole bunch of other problems are going to surface throughout the plant. Batch sizes will change, assembly procedures will have to change. You'll begin to have problems with your suppliers. I know this sounds like opening Pandora's Box, and in a way it is. Every solution is tomorrow's problem as you *strive for continuous improvement.*

"We haven't finished your SMED training yet. Consider this: Can you simplify the previous internal setup steps? You have 255 minutes of internal setup. Let's think about what this is telling us. If you now have a setup that is half of the previous setup, what does that tell you?"

Gus was getting interested. He said, "Well, if you reduce the setup time by half, you don't need to make as many parts as before to break even. I can see that if we needed to make 1000 parts to break even before, we'll probably need fewer parts now. Maybe only 500."

Phil acknowledged this positive input from Gus. "Right on, Gus! That is your name, isn't it?" Gus nodded.

Phil went on, "The actual formula to figure the right size to break even is called the economic order quantity or EOQ. So we know that if we reduce setup, we reduce the economic order quantity. We can plug the new setup time into the EOQ equation and you'll get a good handle on the lot size required to break even.

"Don't get me distracted. Let's get back to the basics of SMED. Dr. Elbie or someone else will get into the EOQ stuff. Let's see what we have here. After we separate internal from external setup, we try to simplify internal setup. Any ideas on how we can do that?"

Jim was quite engrossed in the discussion but hadn't said very much. Then he said, "Phil, I think we could simplify the internal setup a lot just by paying attention to the fact that we're measuring it. Once we start measuring the setup details, I'm sure we will all have ideas on how to simplify the process. It will come to us."

I had to agree with that. When Dr. Elbie was talking about the Hawthorne Effect, he was implying something like that. I think I would pay more attention if I knew I was being measured.

Jim went on. "On that list in front of us, I bet we could take those first two steps and cut the 55 minutes to no more than 20 minutes; 55 minutes is entirely too long." Jim looked in my direction and asked, "Do you agree with that or am I just being optimistic?"

I thought a second and said, "Jim, I wasn't even paying attention to what I was doing. I think if I did, I could do it in 20 minutes without too much pressure. I could probably cut it to 5 minutes if I had a cart to put the tools in that I remove from the machine. You know, I'm talking about a cart with a holder for each of the tools. I saw something like that in one of the tooling magazines. We could probably make one up in about an hour by using some plywood. It would fit neatly on one of the shop carts that we have."

Mr. Grimes said, "That's a very good suggestion. Jim, take that suggestion and make it work. Have one cart bring him his tools and another one take them away. I'll bet that'll work. Give it a try and see what happens."

Mr. Grimes leaned back in his chair with his hands behind his head as if he had just climbed Mt. Everest. "This is fun," he said. "Keep up the good work, Phil."

Phil immediately responded, "Hey, these aren't my ideas. They were *his* and Jim's," as he pointed to Jim and me.

The New Turnaround

"So I hope you guys and gals are getting the drift of this." Everyone nodded yes.

What was amazing was that everyone, including Roland and Buck, was paying close attention.

Phil went on, "After you go through the second step of the SMED process, simplification, then you look at the third step and that is all you have to do to optimize internal setup. Remember, there are three steps to SMED: 1. separate 2. simplify 3. optimize.

"By optimize, I mean things like quick changeover devices. A good example is the ball lock."

Phil explained that a ball lock is a good device to fasten a vise into position on the machines to very tight tolerances. A ball lock allowed you to lock a plate into position on a milling machine bed by merely turning a hex nut one-fourth of a full turn. The quarter turn locking allows the operators to change plates and vises very quickly on the machines. He thought that .002 inches repeatability for a vise fastened into position with four ball locks was pretty reasonable.

Then Phil broke up the class and Gus and Tony and several other people hung around to talk about the ball lock. Phil had a couple of samples for everyone to play with, and play they did.

It was fun to see everyone interested in learning about these things. When we went out to the shop, Gus and Tony came over to my machine and talked about how they could develop a system for quick changeover using the ball locks. They were convinced that they could do this and convert all the machines in the plant over a weekend.

Whatever it was, Gus and Tony and Buck and all the employees who were usually pretty negative were suddenly showing interest. They were convinced that Quality Pump could be saved and they were going to lead the charge.

13

When we walked into class the next morning, everyone was excited. Mr. Grimes was there about fifteen minutes early. He wanted to find out where we were going next. He was going to push for the change. No one was going to get in his way. Someone quoted him as saying, "I see light at the other end of the tunnel and I'm sure that it's not a train. It really is the light at the other end."

Phil and the class talked through the setup concept for about thirty minutes and everyone was convinced that we should make the commitment to this changeover. Before long, Phil asked, "Has anyone thought of the size of the waste involved here?"

Mr. Grimes immediately said, "I have. And you know what it is? It is that our setup accounts for over 35% of our net production hours. Jim and I have been going over our numbers for the last three months. Our setup is over 35% of our direct labor charge. If we can reduce it to 10% of our net production hours, we can generate 25% more work from the factory with no additional expenses other than materials. If we do this, we're going to be healthy very soon.

"And do you know what else? We can respond to orders more quickly because we won't have the long setups and we'll have a reduced inventory."

Phil continued, "You're right on that issue, Mr. Grimes. If you are currently making pumps in batches of one thousand units because that's the way your manufacturing is designed, then the advantage of the reduced setup is that batches of production can be smaller. There is a tradeoff that has to take place here, though. Does anyone know what it is?"

Andrew immediately jumped in. "Yessir, I know! It's this. If you do more setups, you may not get any more production out of the plant. There is an optimum number of setups to do each week to get the most out of the operation given the setup time and the order rate for various products."

"Very good, Andrew," Phil noted. "This is the tricky part and we've got plenty of time to worry about it. The final decision will depend on the strategy of the marketing department in deciding what products

The New Turnaround

will bring in the most revenue. We'll need to understand that before too long.

"Let's talk about inventory. How big is your inventory, Mr. Grimes? Let's talk about raw materials, work in process and finished inventory. If you want to eliminate waste in inventory, we have to start right here. How does your inventory break out?"

Mr. Grimes thought a second. Then he said, "As of last Friday, we had $2.1 million of raw materials, castings, steel, miscellaneous parts; $1.7 million of work in process and $1.7 million of finished inventory for a total of around $5.5 million."

Then Phil asked, "Does anyone other than Mr. Grimes know why this inventory is costing him money?"

Andrew jumped in. "He pays taxes to the state on the physical inventory. And the Fed gets in there, too. More than anything, inventory ties up his money. If he has inventory, he doesn't have money for machines or any other uses for the business."

"Very good, Andrew," Phil said. "So we have a waste of stock and inventory, which is directly attributable to your inefficient operation. How does reduced setup help this issue?"

Roland had been quiet for the last several days. Today he said, "First of all, reduced setup means that you can run jobs in smaller lots. If you have smaller lots, you'll reduce work in process. If we can get products out the door in a more timely fashion, with shorter setups, we won't have such a big inventory of finished goods. That's really the killer because we can never forecast the products accurately. That damned MRP system is terrible and it certainly doesn't predict the buying habits of our customers. The quick setup will make us more responsive to the market and our finished inventory will drop.

"And I think that if we play our cards right, we can reduce the amount of raw materials that we'll need because we'll only need those materials to meet our short-term requirements. I think that about covers it."

Everyone was listening to Roland. He was very good, very persuasive. He had the gift of gab. If that made a good salesman, then he was a good salesman. And he was very positive about what was going on in the class. I figured that he was finally getting on board.

Phil continued, "The good thing about setup reduction is that if you take an eight-hour setup down to fifteen minutes, then you can make one hundred pieces and still be profitable. You don't have to make 500 units to fill a 200 unit order. If you don't have 300 excess, you have nothing to store or count or pay taxes on. By the way, does anyone know the optimum batch size?"

I couldn't believe that this guy was making such sense. He didn't have the credentials of Dr. Elbie, yet he really knew his business. I knew the answer, so I raised my hand. Phil called on me and I said, "One."

"Exactly!" Phil said. "We strive to make setup zero or as close to it as possible. That way you can make one unit at a time. You could be totally responsive to the market and Roland would sure love that." He glanced in Roland's direction and everyone turned. Roland nodded an emphatic yes. "If you could do that, you wouldn't need big warehouses to store finished goods or WIP. If an hour after a customer called, his product could be in the delivery truck, you wouldn't need to carry any inventory at all. You would just build it for him right then and there.

"Not only would you not need a finished-goods warehouse, you also wouldn't need to keep six months' worth of raw materials. And those people who're not adding value to the company by moving and counting that inventory could be given jobs that do add value. Keep a month's worth of raw materials and as the orders come in and the raw materials are used, order some more."

Phil continued, "I'll probably be here teaching the class for a couple more days. After that, I'll be on the shop floor for about three weeks assisting you in setup changes. If you have any questions or ideas, please feel free to talk to me and I'll help you in any way I can.

"Our company also has a lending library. We have many books on setup, plant management and other stuff. We'll be happy to lend you any of the materials you might need. Just see me after class.

"Now, if you would break up into your teams, I'd like you to look at whatever current projects you are working on. Using this example as a guide," he held up my setup data, "see how you can apply these principles to your particular problem."

We broke up along team lines. Soon we realized that the people from the office team had nothing to do, so we asked them to divvy themselves up among the production teams. Our team drew Roland. He was fascinated by the idea of setup reduction because if we could reduce setup time, he could deliver to the customer much earlier. It would give us a real jump on the competition.

He said, "If we could use this to shorten the time between taking and filling an order, we'd sell many more products. We lose orders

The New Turnaround

because other companies with comparable products can deliver them sooner than we can."

We decided to meet again after work. I told everyone that I had to be on the road by five o'clock, so we agreed to watch the time.

After work that afternoon we were really surprised. Roland joined us for our afternoon bull session and he brought Bonnie in with him. Bonnie seemed to really warm up to the shop people since the training started. She didn't seem to be afraid of us like she was before.

We met in the classroom. Dr. Elbie and Phil were still there looking over some paperwork. As Dr. Elbie prepared to leave, Phil asked if he could sit in on our brainstorming session, saying, "I'll be here strictly as an observer; you'll make all the decisions. If you need any further information, I'll try to provide it."

We were just getting started when the women from the assembly team came into the classroom. Patty, the team leader, said, "Oh, we didn't realize this room was being used. We can have our meeting in the lunchroom." We told her that there was plenty of room and that they could share the room with us. She asked what we were working on and we told her. She said it was pretty interesting. Then she went over and joined her own group.

That afternoon we mostly talked about the idea of moving an XS machine into our cell. We all thought it was a good idea, but we kept coming up with reasons to shoot it down.

I said, "It seems to me that the programming wouldn't be so difficult, but I think we're going to have a war getting Bernard to investigate the idea. I just can't see how they are going to agree to put a three hundred thousand dollar machine in a cell where it will sit idle part of the time."

Roland said, "They'll agree if we can prove to Mr. Grimes that it makes economic sense. Like I said, we're getting killed by the competition. Other companies have to be developing systems for air conditioning much like ours. It doesn't matter if we have the best product if we can't deliver it in a timely manner. Our potential customers will just buy from someone else."

Roland agreed to work with us on the sales figures to help us justify moving the machine. Phil said he had some books that might help us and that he would bring them the next day. We broke up a few minutes before five and I headed out.

On the drive home, I kept coming back to the setup. What if we divided the plant into specific product lines and put the assembly right next to the production machines? Would it work? There would be a significant reduction in the waste of having to carry the casings all over the plant. We could carry the product from raw material to a finished and tested unit in one area. It would save serious time. It made a lot of sense to me. Then I started to chuckle because I was starting to sound like Phil.

As I pulled into the driveway, Buddy was shooting baskets at the hoop. He was beginning to show a good eye for the basket. He loved all sports and loved to fish with me. There was a movie coming to town about fishing in Montana and I was going to take Buddy over the weekend. I read about it in a magazine and got a copy of the book at a local bookstore. I read it as soon as I got home. Sandy noticed that I was reading more and watching less television since joining Quality Pump. She really liked that and was beginning to feel comfortable with the changes taking place at home and at work.

14

I got to work early the next morning because I wanted to see what books were available. Dr. Elbie was stacking cartons of books and videotapes along the front wall of the classroom. Phil was wheeling in a hand truck full of boxes of books. "Good morning," I said.

Dr. Elbie replied, "Good morning; see anything that might interest you?"

I told him I was interested in SMED, and he handed me a book by a Japanese guy. I signed the book out and walked over to my chair.

I started comparing notes with other people in my work area. We were all enthusiastic about what was going on. We were finding wastes in places we never even considered. Some of our ideas were starting to get implemented and that was exciting.

Kelly, one of the machinists, had an idea to hang our working drawings above the workbench. We calculated that it would save at least $30,000 a year in rework because the drawings wouldn't get oil on them, like they did when we put them on oily benches. At least two bad runs a month were attributable to misreads of drawings that had dimensions labels smeared with oil. Each run cost about $1250. She mounted a couple of sticks at the ends of the bench and strung a wire between them. She put half a dozen spring clips on the wire. It was just like a clothesline on our workbench. The clips hung on there and could slide back and forth. We could hang our drawings with the clips. That kept them off the bench, so they didn't get dirty and we didn't have to move the drawings every time we wanted to do something on the bench. It was a good idea and it made the work a lot smoother.

Things like that were getting put into place. Simple things, but they made the work a lot easier. As Dr. Elbie kept repeating, we were finding a simple project and doing it.

In fact, ideas were coming in from all over the place. Even the receptionist was contributing a lot of ideas. Apparently, she was quite a pistol. She was getting into the classes, had ideas for all the teams in her class, and was very excited about her ideas being implemented.

She came up with a coding system for the custom orders on the new work sheet. She and Bernard worked together and put it into the computer and it was great! One of the guys walked all the way around the building so he could enter the factory through the reception area because he wanted to say good morning to her and thank her for her great ideas.

I heard that Mr. Grimes had to take over for his secretary when she went to class. Gus said Mr. Grimes would never have done anything like that before.

As the classes kept going, the line of distinction between workers and managers was slowly beginning to disappear. The isolation or separation between the different departments was also disappearing. Having Roland and Bonnie on our team was good. They were from sales and marketing and we were from the shop. It made them one of "us." And in a strange way I think it made "us" one of "them."

By the third day, Phil was wearing tennis shoes and T-shirts to class. One day he wore a black T-shirt with a picture of a wild boar's head on it. In a circle around the boar's head was written, In Hogs We Trust.

Buck saw that shirt and loved it. He went to Phil after class and said, "What do you ride?"

Phil replied, "A Harley."

Buck was jazzed. "An American Hog, right on!" As he walked away he muttered, "Right on!"

We spent the class time looking at ways to reduce setup. Both Dr. Elbie and Phil gave lectures on ways this could be accomplished. The class came up with new ideas for each new concept that was introduced. Some of them seemed kind of ridiculous and some of them made good sense. Everyone was willing to listen and it seemed to bring out a positive response all around.

We kept coming back to putting the programmers on the shop floor. Bernard was adamant that the programmers belonged in their office. Jim said, "When I first started in manufacturing, I was straight out of college. As a plant superintendent, I thought I needed an office. After a while, I moved my office out onto the shop floor because that was where the action was. It was exciting to be out there with all the noise and smells. Then I was really part of the creative process. The creative process for me doesn't end at the drawing board. It starts when we get the drawing to the shop floor."

It seemed like a little chink in Bernard's armor had been removed. Bernard had a lot of respect for Jim because in addition to being plant manager, he was also a good programmer.

The most surprising reaction to the classes on SMED was from Gus. He argued a couple of times that we already had those kinds of processes in place, but you could tell from the way he was paying attention that he was interested in the idea.

Dr. Elbie pointed out that he realized we were already using some of the ideas he presented, but we shouldn't rest on our laurels. He said, "What we expect is continuous improvement. After this training is done, you'll be equipped to carry on with this idea. Up to now you've made improvements in a haphazard manner. Some have worked out great and some have been disasters. After we leave, some improvements will work out great and some will still be disasters. The difference is that after a disaster you'll be able to pick yourself up and know what you need to do to get back on track, and try again. When you can do that, work becomes exciting. You'll never know what will happen next. On any given day you can make a quantum leap in productivity!

"Before I let you go, I would like to give you another tool to think about in your analysis. This tool is called the 80/20 Rule or the Pareto Principle, and here is how it works. I bring it up here because it relates to issues that you are trying to solve.

"Consider this curve," said Dr. Elbie as he projected the following graph up on the wall.

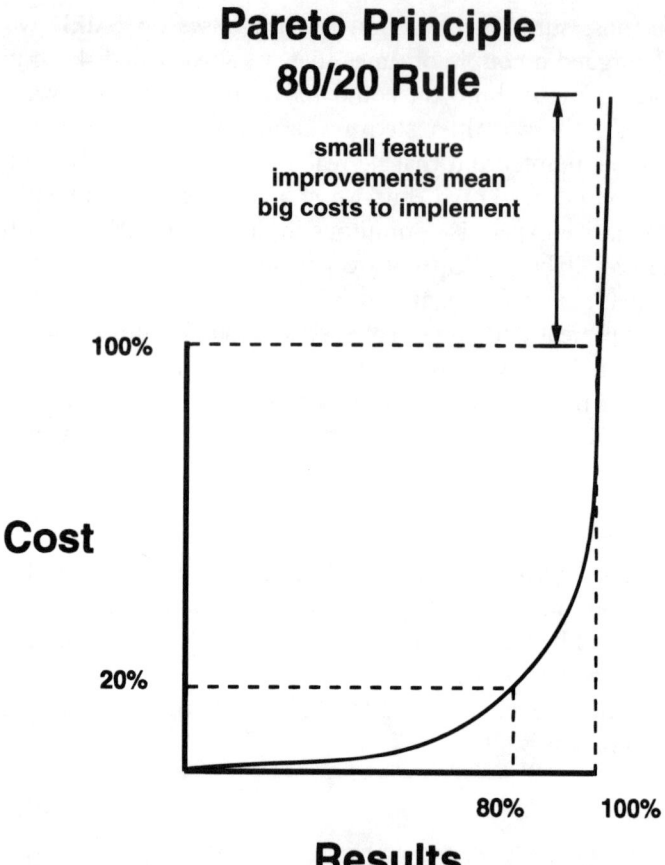

"If I identify a waste of $100,000 and it costs me $25,000 to buy a piece of equipment to solve the problem, can I spend less money and get rid of any of the waste? It turns out that in almost all cases, we can get rid of 80% of the waste by spending only 20% of what it would cost to eliminate 100% of the waste. Does that make sense?"

Bonnie was intrigued, "You mean to tell me, Dr. Elbie, that if we come up with a solution, then you would ask us to solve it by spending only 20% of our recommended costs of implementation. Is that what you are saying?"

"Absolutely! Doesn't Mr. Grimes do that anyway? Doesn't he always tell you to think about spending money as if it were your own." Bonnie nodded her agreement. "What we are asking you to do is think of problems as being variable in the amount of money that you spend.

The New Turnaround

You can always spend lots of money but does it get you what you need at the time? Maybe you can spend less money and move the solution forward. Stop the bleeding, if that's what is called for. It turns out that as time goes by, the problem looks different. In six months, after spending only 20% of the dollars that were projected earlier, you may have a better understanding of the problem and be able to make a more informed decision.

"I believe that this thinking will help all of you analyze your problems differently. You may solve the problem for a few dollars by moving equipment around or changing the process without having to make big investments. That is the goal of this training. We are trying to show you that there may be any number of ways to get 80% of the way into the solution by spending fewer dollars. And it usually turns out that to reach that last 20% is very expensive. Does everyone understand this?"

Buck was intrigued, "You mean to tell me that if I can solve a problem by spending $20,000 to eliminate $100,000 of waste, that I could just as well spend $4,000 and eliminate $80,0000 of waste. Would Mr. Grimes be for this?"

Dr. Elbie looked at Mr. Grimes. "You bet I would! I would always be willing to invest $4,000 to help solve a bothersome $100,000 problem, especially if the $4,000 gets rid of $80,000 of the problem. I guess I do this without thinking. But you made me aware of why I do it. By the way, Jack, doesn't this concept apply to other areas of our business as well?"

"Does anyone have any input here? Can the 80/20 Rule be applied to other problems? If so, how?"

Roland immediately jumped in, "You know, 80% of my problems come from 20% of my customers. That I know for sure. And 80% of my revenues come from 20% of my customers."

Buck moaned, "And 80% of my late shipments are caused by 20% of the trucking companies that we use. I was just looking at some numbers here; I see 78% of my late shipments were caused by 16% of the trucking companies. I guess that is the 78/16 Rule."

Everyone laughed at Buck's humor and then conversation developed around the many applications of this principle. It was really interesting how it worked.

Dr. Elbie concluded, "The most interesting consequence of the 80/20 Rule in reality is probably that it allows you to spend a little money, get rid of some of the problem, and after several months a new variation of the problem comes up. But it is a different problem, and you didn't spend that additional 80% to get there. In essence, what this does is get you to put out only as much money as needed to stop the bleeding, because we know other problems will arise that require the bigger investments."

Dr. Elbie then went on, "OK, that does it for today."

For me, the class ended too soon that day. I had things I wanted to discuss, but we ran out of time. I jotted down some notes so I would remember, and went out to work. At break time Patty came over to Billy and me. She said that if we could meet with her team that afternoon, they would show us some good ideas about the new valve assembly.

That afternoon we all met in the classroom after work. As we walked in, Tony was in a heated discussion with one of his team-members. ". . . we're putting in overtime and we're not getting paid for it!"

When we were seated Tony said, "Kelly brought up a problem that I'm sure has crossed all of your minds. She was wondering about all the time that the team is putting in after work. She asked whether we were going to be paid for it. I don't think we ought to ask for any overtime pay.

"Grimes is spending a lot of money to provide this training and keep the plant in operation. As most of you know, I have enough years in so that I could retire today. So it really doesn't matter to me if this plant stays open or not—I'll still get my pension! But you young people have a real stake in this plant.

"I'll tell you this: Ed was right when he said we shouldn't complain about the little things. So what if we invest a few hours we're not paid for! What you're doing is investing in your future. You're going to be paid a hundred-fold in job security, and unless we do this we probably won't have jobs. Just get off the bullshit and get with it, Kelly."

Kelly didn't have much to say after that. Man, I couldn't believe the change in Tony's attitude.

That afternoon, while we were kicking around the idea of a dedicated cell, we ran into another brick wall. The ACME and the XS machines didn't use the same vise system. The process we were considering would entail moving parts in process from one machine to another. It would be a setup nightmare to get the required vises in the same relative position on both machines. The only thing we could come up with was to dedicate an ACME 1000 to the cell in addition to the XS 2040 machine, but we knew that management would never go for idling two machines. We were almost ready to give up on the idea.

As we began the discussion, we mentioned our problem to the other members of the team and Bonnie asked if the machines used the same computer controller. We told her that they did, and she said "I may have a solution for this problem, let me check something out."

The next morning I found Bonnie, Tony and Jim already in the classroom. Tony said to me, "Come here and check this out." When I joined them, I saw they were all looking at a machining magazine.

I caught the tail end of Bonnie's explanation ". . . So, if we work the XY axis from the same point on both machines, we could just change the baseplate that has the vises already mounted."

I looked at the ad in the magazine. It was instantly clear to me that Bonnie was on to a solution. She had found something called a ball lock baseplate system. This would allow us to mount the vises on the baseplate and then we could move the baseplate from the XS to the ACME without having to set up the vises again. It looked like once the machine was set up to accept the ball lock system we could change the baseplate in less than a minute!

Bonnie said, "I haven't checked the actual price of the system, but I talked with my dad over the weekend and he thought the cost would be less than five hundred dollars per machine."

I asked Bonnie, "How do you know about this kind of stuff?"

Bonnie smiled and said, "My dad was an engineer for years in Detroit. I grew up around this stuff. When I originally applied here it was for a design job. I have a degree in mechanical engineering. They didn't have any openings in engineering, but they offered me a job in sales, so I took it."

Bonnie was an engineer; that was a shocker. In class that day we talked about this ball lock system some more. It was the solution after all, and we all knew it. When Phil originally mentioned it, we didn't think of using it in this way.

Phil said, "I think this ball lock system will work pretty well for you. Like I said before, we're great believers in low-tech solutions. Based on my experience in machining, I'm a great believer in jigs or fixtures to hold a product in a fixed position. Every new setup is an opportunity to make your business more efficient. You can build a jig to do one operation. Let each jig be dedicated to a specific job. That way you can have the setup crew prepare each job ahead of time. You never wait for equipment that is tied up in another job." You could almost see the light bulb over Gus's head. He realized that he could build a separate set of jigs and fixtures for every job. His crew would be responsible for them and setup would definitely be affected in a positive way. Gus was obviously excited.

15

Jim came over to me just before class on Monday morning. He told me that Mr. Grimes was very upset. Apparently Mr. Grimes had come into the parking lot at about 6:00 A.M. He had a meeting with Dr. Elbie before class. As Jim told it, Mr. Grimes drove through the snow into the parking lot and noticed something under the light in the distance but he couldn't make out what it was. As he got closer to the shop door he recognized the figure as a man, but under all the clothing he couldn't tell who it was.

Mr. Grimes told Jim later that it was only after he opened the shop door and he and the figure rushed inside that Mr. Grimes recognized who it was. It was Ramon, who worked in the assembly area as a boxer and clean-up man. Ramon stood shivering near the door. Water was dripping on the concrete as the snow on his clothes started to melt. His teeth chattered and his lips had turned blue.

Jim said that Mr. Grimes and Ramon went into the lunchroom. As Mr. Grimes made coffee he asked Ramon what he was doing there at that time of the day. Work didn't start for over an hour.

Ramon apparently was waiting for Mike Cain and had been standing in the parking lot since 5:40 when his wife dropped him off. Ramon's wife took their family car to her job at the big hotel out on the highway.

The fresh aroma of coffee filled the lunchroom. Mr. Grimes rushed over to the pot and got the first cup for Ramon.

Mr. Grimes talked with Ramon for a while and found that he knew that Mr. Grimes was going to meet with Dr. Elbie that morning. Mr. Grimes asked Ramon how he liked the classes. Ramon acknowledged that he liked them.

Mr. Grimes also found that Ramon's brother and cousin also worked at the company. They had come directly from Mexico with papers and had been in this country for two years. Ramon's brother, Pablo, worked in supply, and his cousin worked in shipping and on the loading dock.

They all liked the classes and their chances for opportunity in the United States. Ramon was a laborer in Mexico and would be a laborer all his life, if he stayed there. Here, he and his family could go to school. They could learn and make their lives much better.

Mr. Grimes called to Jim as he walked by the lunchroom door. While Jim waited at the door, Mr. Grimes said to Ramon, "I will personally see that you don't have to wait outside again. Thank you for visiting with me. Are you warm yet?"

Ramon answered, "Yes, Señor Grimes, I am now. The coffee helped. Gracias."

Mr. Grimes took Jim into his office. Jim told me that as they sat down, Mr. Grimes asked, "Why was that man standing outside this morning? For heaven's sake, it's twelve degrees below zero, and the wind is blowing like hell! He was out there for over half an hour. He could have frozen to death!"

Jim replied, "It's Mike Cain's responsibility. He hasn't been cooperating with the plan to come in early. He figures that if there is no early morning inspection, he doesn't have to come in. To tell you the truth, he has been fighting all these changes tooth and nail. I've been getting complaints from the new teams that he won't work with them on inspection. A big reason we aren't getting the setup time down is that he won't jump to do the inspection when it's needed.

"Jack has brought in one of his associates to talk with him. They have had a few sessions, but it hasn't done any good yet."

Jim left, and Mr. Grimes went to see Dr. Elbie. Dr. Elbie was sitting at one of the tables looking at some papers. Mr. Grimes greeted him and said, "How's it going? Things are really cooking in this place. I have to admit it, Jack, this VAP system really works! I can't believe everyone's enthusiasm.

"I'm sorry for being a little late. I had a little problem to take care of. By the way, have you heard anyone complaining about Mike Cain?"

"Yes, I have. People are reluctant to say anything about him because he goes back a long way with you. He's fighting the process all the way. He's the most negative guy in the whole company. He just doesn't want to change."

Dr. Elbie went on, "It's starting to get in the way of his group. In fact, that's why I asked to get together with you this morning. You have to face that problem directly. You can't avoid it a second longer. If you do, he'll weaken the program. People will sense it as a sign of weakness on your part and your unwillingness to take appropriate action with a friend or a long-time employee. He clearly has to get on board."

The New Turnaround

Mr. Grimes apologized for Mike and said, "Jack, Mike was the reason that I was delayed getting up here. He had one of his crew get in early and he didn't show up. Ramon was waiting in the cold. I can't believe Mike did that. Mike has always been a good employee and I've always had a lot of confidence in him."

Dr. Elbie interrupted him momentarily, "You don't have to shoot him. You just have to get him to support the changes we are making."

Mr. Grimes went on, "That's the problem. Most of the changes being made are changes to systems he personally put in place a number of years ago. I know Mike pretty well, and I'm sure that he's taking all of the changes as personal attacks against him. You can have anyone you want talk to him, but that's what it boils down to. Mike tends to be insulted every time someone points out problems in the way anything that he had a hand in is done. Most of our systems were put in by him years ago and have just grown like Topsie.

"There has been no rhyme or reason for much of it. And to be quite frank, I never paid much attention. It wasn't until last week that I realized that the costs of keeping the system unchanged were phenomenal. There is no way we were going to make it without this training. Mike is one of my most trusted employees and a very good friend, but I don't see how to solve this short of firing him. He won't change."

Dr. Elbie was listening intently to everything Mr. Grimes was saying and asked matter of factly, "Have you ever asked Mike to do something he didn't want to do?"

"Yes, of course," Mr. Grimes responded. He continued, "He will always fight it to the limit and then capitulate in the end, but this training activity is somehow different. He has put his heart and soul into the company and doesn't want anything to change."

"I think you know what you need to do. Talk with Mike. Give him a direct order and get him on board. If he fails to do what you say, you have no choice. Try to get him to participate on one of the teams. Maybe you could even move him to another class. Saving face is very difficult for a man in his position. He is trying to do a good job and in the past he has always come through for you. Regardless, he must not get in the way of the changes taking place. If he does anything to interfere, you have to take care of him immediately. We have had at least one guy like him in every company where we have done training. At some point, he is either in or he is out. He fishes or he cuts bait. He has no choice in that."

Mr. Grimes was pained. He loved Mike and would hate to terminate him, but he knew it was coming. Mike was stubborn and wouldn't give in easily.

Class started and Mr. Grimes excused himself about half-way into it. He went to his office and asked his secretary to get Mike Cain. After a few minutes, Mike walked into Mr. Grimes' office and sat down. Mr. Grimes got up and shut the door. Mike had been around a long time and knew that the closed door meant a serious discussion with Mr. Grimes. He rarely closed his door. Mike knew what was coming.

Mr. Grimes looked across the desk at Mike and said, "Mike, I came in early this morning. Did you know that?"

"Yes, I heard."

"When I got here, Ramon was standing outside in the cold. It was twelve degrees below zero and he was left standing out there alone. If I hadn't come along, Lord knows what would have happened. What's going on? That was totally irresponsible. You really do know better than that."

Mike knew that Mr. Grimes was angry. He was very direct and he always had been. Mike was fidgeting in his seat. He didn't have a defense and he knew it. "I'm sorry, John, I guess I am just irritated with having to get up so early in the morning. I don't see why we can't get the work done so that I don't have to come in early. You are making me suffer so that everyone else can duff it during the day. I don't like having to cover for them."

Mr. Grimes was really upset now. "Mike, don't you ever learn? You almost caused a man to freeze to death because of your petty bullshit. I need your support and you aren't giving it. Are you going to get on board or am I going to move this train to the next station without you? What's it going to be?"

Mike had never seen Mr. Grimes so angry. He was cornered. He didn't want to support Dr. Elbie and all this change. He liked it the way it was. As he sat there, Mr. Grimes barked, "Mike, I'm waiting for your response."

Mike looked down as he began to speak. "I'm sorry, John. I just don't want to play. This is all a crock of shit and you know it. People are going to get jazzed about this for a few weeks, maybe even a few months, and it will be back to the same old shit. I've been with you a long time and I don't see you changing to the kind of guy who will make this work. I think that everyone is in for a rude awakening and I

The New Turnaround

don't want to be here when that happens. I guess I should resign now while we are still friends. I can't get behind this program."

Mr. Grimes answered rather sternly. "So that's your response, you're resigning?"

Mike nodded his affirmation. "I'm sorry it's come to this but I'll get out of here as soon as you want me to go."

Mr. Grimes said, "I would like you to go immediately. I'll go down with you to the payroll department and get that squared away. I'll make sure all your pension and other monies get worked out fairly. I'm committed to make this process work and I don't want anyone to get in the way. I'm sorry that you couldn't get on board, but I will have no insubordination while we are trying to make this work. After you leave, I will go down to Ramon and apologize for you. And I am going to give Ramon the rest of the day off."

They got up, walked down to payroll, and Mike Cain was history. Mr. Grimes felt miserable about it, but he knew there was no alternative.

Mr. Grimes returned to his office and waited for his 10:00 A.M. appointment. He was going to interview a man who used to work at Osgood's. The appointment was on time. Mr. Grimes talked with the man for a little bit, reviewed his resume in great detail and was very impressed with his credentials. He got up and took him on a tour of the plant. As he walked out to our area, I looked at him. I couldn't believe it—Mr. Grimes had *Darth Vader* with him! There were several of us back at Quality Pump who would have participated in his hanging, but why was he here? Mr. Grimes wasn't going to hire him was he? Oh, my God, what was he doing?

As Mr. Grimes walked him around the facility, Jim came out of nowhere and shook hands with the man. They smiled at each other and seemed quite friendly. Mr. Grimes stayed a few minutes and then took off. Jim spent a little time at his desk with the man, then stood up and headed over in my direction. I couldn't believe this. Why was Jim bringing him over to me? I hated his guts for what he did to us and to Charlie. This was terrible.

Apparently, Jim knew this guy, because they were real chummy. Why were they bringing him in here? He was trouble. He would destroy this organization just like he destroyed Osgood's. They arrived at my station and I didn't feel very well. As they approached, Jim asked me if I was alright. I acknowledged that I was, and he proceeded to introduce me, "This is Calvin Jackson. He used to work at Osgood's. Oh, you two probably know each other."

"Yes, we both worked at Osgood's. I expected to retire from there. Calvin just worked there a little while. Nice to see you again." The sarcasm in my voice came through loud and clear. "My friend, Charlie, told me say hello to you if we ever ran into each other."

Calvin was clearly bothered by my reaction. I couldn't have cared less. Calvin represented the worst in American management and I wasn't going to miss my opportunity. We certainly didn't need his kind here. He would destroy any good that Dr. Elbie was doing. Why was he here?

Calvin said, "I heard about Charlie. Was he a friend of yours?"

"Yes, he *was*. I was a third generation employee at Osgood's and Charlie was a good friend of my father's and mine. He taught me a lot about machining. In fact, we interviewed together for this job. I got a job and he didn't. I would appreciate it if you left me alone. I really don't like you or what you did to Osgood's. It was immoral. You killed Charlie's spirit and you almost killed mine."

I turned and went back to my work. I hated Calvin. As far as I was concerned he was the devil personified. He had destroyed a lot of people's lives and he probably felt no remorse. What I did was wrong but they can't bring him in here. He would be bad for what we were doing.

Jim came over to me after lunch. He was angry. He told me that I was rude and that I had insulted his friend. I told Jim that if that guy was his friend he ought to examine his conscience. What Calvin did at Osgood's was unpardonable. And Jim had no right to judge me. I had lost my job as a result of that man and I was entitled to my own opinion whether Jim liked it or not. Jim did not back down. He was mad. I was madder. Jim started to yell at me. I yelled back. Everyone in the place was looking at us and I was right in Jim's face.

Jim turned and left. He went over to his desk and sat there for the longest time. My setup was going slow and I had a hard time concentrating on what I was doing. It was not like me to yell at someone. Whenever I did, I usually got over it quickly. This time my anger lingered. I really did not want to see Darth Vader at our facility.

Jim came over just before quitting time. He asked me quietly, "Have you calmed down yet?"

I answered, "Jim, to be quite frank with you, no. No way. As you can gather, I get quite emotional about my experience at Osgood's. I

The New Turnaround

was unemployed for a long time because of 'your friend.' I resent what he did to me and all the people at Osgood's. I can't tell you that I am sorry for yelling at you earlier. I'm not. That's the way I feel. I've been through a lot of stuff in the last six months and seeing him was not a very warm moment."

Jim said, "I'm sorry for bringing him over to you. I forgot about how close you were to Charlie and how long your family had been associated with Osgood's. I should have known you would react that way. It is only natural, I guess. I'm sorry for upsetting you. Forgive me for my stupidity, OK?" As he left, he said, "I'll see you tomorrow in class."

As I drove home, I thought intently about my discussion with Jim and Darth Vader. Normally I am not so rude. Darth Vader had caused so much pain and suffering after he took over at Osgood's that it was very difficult to find any good in the man. He had closed the plant that Dad and Grandpa had been at all their working days. He had put Charlie and me on the unemployment lines. And more than likely, his action had led to Charlie's death.

As I was pulling into the driveway, it suddenly struck me. Maybe he was just following orders and someone else had called all the shots. I pulled the truck to a stop and just sat in the cab for a few minutes thinking about this situation. I heard a loud knock on the cab window. It was Buddy. He had his football. He wanted to toss it around with me.

I got out of the cab with my mind way down the line. I was very distracted as I played with Buddy. I kept thinking about that afternoon and what Darth Vader was doing there. Buddy was commenting on my throwing. I wasn't aiming well and, more importantly, I wasn't very talkative. Buddy had a good arm and threw one right at my head. I wasn't paying attention and the ball hit me square on the forehead. I went down for the count. Buddy started to laugh but then got concerned when he realized that I might be hurt.

I laughed, but boy, did I have a goose egg on my forehead! We continued passing for a few more minutes and then Sandy called and said I had a phone call. I tossed the ball back to Buddy and said, "Why don't we go in? I bet Mom has dinner on the table or is nearly ready."

I raced Buddy to the back porch. He won, and then we raced into the house to the sound of Sandy, "No running!" We stopped, I gave Sandy a kiss and picked up the phone. It was Jim, the plant manager.

"Have you eaten dinner yet?"

I responded formally, "I just got in and we were about to sit down. What's the matter?"

"Well," he said, "I would like to take you to dinner with Calvin, Mr. Grimes and Dr. Elbie. If you would like to join us, I can be by your place in about an hour. We'll eat down at The Shanty. Do you need to check first?"

I thought a second and asked Jim where he was. He told me that he was at work with Mr. Grimes and Dr. Elbie. I asked, "Could I call you right back? I don't know what's on the agenda at home here. I just got in and Sandy has dinner ready. She may not be pleased. Let me talk to her and I'll call you right back."

Jim paused before he answered, "OK, no problem. Call us on Mr. Grimes' line." And he gave me Mr. Grimes' private line at the office.

Sandy was interested in the phone call. The kids were all excited and Mickey wanted me to hold him. I grabbed him from Sandy and told her about the phone call and what had happened at work.

"Oh, my God," she sighed, "they're going to fire you. They're going to fire you, aren't they?"

I joked, "At least they can do it to me on a full stomach."

I thought a few minutes and asked Sandy, "Is my shirt ironed?"

She gave me that look, as if to say, What do you think I did after I washed it, stuff it in the drawer like you would? In a very serious voice, she asked, "What could they possibly want? Why would they call you like this? Do you think they are going to fire you? No one ever invited you to dinner before. Is this the new way to fire someone?"

I put my hand up and firmly said, "Stop, Sandy. I don't know what they want. I would like to go to dinner and find out. What have I got to lose?" I called Jim back and accepted his invitation. He was pleased. In spite of our earlier differences, I liked Jim and knew he was a straight shooter. If he had invited me, it must be serious and I owed him that much.

Sandy was nervous as I went out the door to meet Jim. As he opened the front car door, I got in. Dr. Elbie was sitting in the back seat reading something. He acknowledged my entry and continued reading. Jim was all smiles as I shut the door and we headed downtown. As we drove the ten minutes to The Shanty Jim was again apologizing for the afternoon's exchange.

Dr. Elbie was very serious and appeared to be distracted. He had finished the article from the magazine he was reading. I glanced in the back seat as he closed the door and saw that it was the Harvard

Business Review. As we walked into the restaurant, Dr. Elbie finally snapped out of his distraction and rejoined the human race.

Ed Daley was also just arriving. Mr. Grimes and Darth Vader were sitting at the bar drinking Anchor Steam beers. The owner of The Shanty had been in San Francisco some years ago and he really liked Anchor Steam beer. So now he had a regular delivery of the stuff. He attracted local patrons to the bar to drink the fine San Francisco beer. He loved it and we paid dearly. Not a bad deal.

We went over to join Mr. Grimes and were immediately directed to the back room. We all sat down and the waitress took my drink order. I was seated next to Mr. Grimes and Dr. Elbie at the round dinner table. As we all traded amenities, I had none for Darth Vader. Ed asked him about his mother and Darth told Ed that she was doing OK now. The surgery had only slowed her down. She was going to take that cruise she always wanted to take.

That was interesting. So Darth Vader had an earthling mother. As he talked, I noticed a different manner; he'd had an overbearing personality when he was managing Osgood's. Maybe he had mellowed after getting fired. When I had heard that, I couldn't have been a happier fellow. Apparently, Calvin had done a pretty good job selling the assets of Osgood's for maximum dollar value. After doing his job and bringing the plant closure to a rapid end, he was abruptly fired. He was really surprised. He got the old heave-ho just like us. The interesting news to me was that he did the job he was apparently supposed to do and still got axed. It didn't make sense. *Why would they fire him for doing a good job? Unfortunately, as I had been told by my father, doing a good job in America has nothing to do with keeping your job.*

We ordered dinner and the conversation was pretty relaxed. Dr. Elbie was talking about the article that he had read in the Harvard Business Review by Ralph Stayer of the Johnsonville Sausage Company in Wisconsin. Apparently Stayer had been trying to create an employee-involved organization for a long time and had reported his results in the HBR article.

I started to get into these three-letter buzz words pretty good. I had heard about IBM, JIT, MRP, RBI, ERA, SPC, and now HBR. I could just see me talking in a couple of years: "I read about JIT and MRP successes at IBM in the HBR. Their SPC project was a failure." Now that was progress. Life was reduced to nonsensical jibberish. Dr. Elbie called it modern day jabberwocky. I wasn't familiar with that term. Dr.

Elbie told me about the poem by Lewis Carroll, which seemed to make sense but was just gibberish.

Dr. Elbie liked to tell us about stuff like this in class. Most of the employees enjoyed it. It made them feel like the class was on a college level. Andrew, the engineer, told me that he had never had discussions like ours in any of his college classes. They were always lectures and were always boring. Our classes certainly weren't boring.

As dinner progressed, I got to know a little more about Darth Vader. He and Jim had grown up together in a farming area outside of Indianapolis. They had gone to grammar and high schools together. Ed Daley and Darth's mother had known each other from Darth's father's union activities.

After Jim and Calvin, aka Darth Vader, had graduated from high school, Jim went on to Purdue as an industrial engineer and Calvin had gone to the University of Michigan on a General Motors scholarship. When Calvin graduated from Michigan, he was moved into the General Motors program for young engineers with management potential. He quickly moved up the ranks to be a plant manager in one of the GM supplier plants.

He wanted more and decided to go on to get an MBA from the Wharton School of Business, where he had focused on mergers and acquisitions. He joined one of the New York firms specializing in these activities and was immediately sent to Osgood's to run the plant. Once there, he had quickly sized up the situation, and had recommended to the M&A group in New York that they get rid of Osgood's immediately. They took his recommendation and closed the operation at considerable expense after the acquisition. Calvin had performed admirably but had gotten axed. He knew a little about our pain as he had been fired and knew what that did to your head.

As dinner ended, Mr. Grimes sipped his cup of coffee and began to address all of us. He looked at me first and said, "I'm glad that you were able to join us on such short notice. I know that it isn't easy to change a routine but we really wanted you here for this discussion. Thanks again." He then looked at Ed and said, "Ed, I really appreciate you taking time out of your negotiation schedule to help us this evening. We are very grateful for your presence. Thanks again."

Mr. Grimes was smiling as he began, "I have to admit that I wasn't really that excited about spending my money on this program but I can see now that it has been worth every penny up to this point." He looked at Dr. Elbie. Elbie acknowledged his recognition with a nod and Mr. Grimes continued, "Jack tells me that things are going about as expected but that we can make things move even faster with some additional focus at this point. It really makes sense and I would like to implement his suggestion. What I want to do is start the Productivity Review Board tomorrow. I want Ed or one of his representatives active on this board and I want it to be the focus of implementing new ideas. I don't want good ideas to drag on before getting implemented. I want everyone to know that I am serious. Calvin, here," and he pointed to Darth Vader, "has recently completed an assignment at Osgood's."

At that, I almost gagged on my coffee. To say that he had completed an assignment at Osgood's was ridiculous. To say that he had messed with a whole bunch of people's lives was more accurate. He may not have called the shots but he sure pulled the trigger.

I didn't know what this whole thing had to do with me, and then it hit. Mr. Grimes looked directly at me and said, "I want you to work directly with Calvin to make this PRB work. He will be my point man and you will represent the union bargaining unit on this team. The chief steward in our shop thinks you would be a marvelous person to have on the board. I agree. Everyone here agrees. Ed, do you have anything to add?"

Ed didn't miss a beat. "Yes, I do have something to add. This is a new experiment for us. We think it will work. If the union membership contributes to increased productivity in the shop, then we should see our reward in some way at contract negotiation time. The results of this training and the projected improvements will be totally documented. This team will help everyone and I think we want to support it in any way we can." And he turned to me, "I've known your grandpa and your pa for a long time. They think a lot of you, and the strength you showed after getting layed off at Osgood's and losing your good friend, Charlie. We think that you have the character to make this PRB work and we are also endorsing your presence on the committee."

At that moment, Dr. Elbie asked if he could say a few words. Mr. Grimes obliged. Dr. Elbie went on, "I've been watching you," and he looked straight at me, "from the first day I came to you with my crazy ideas. You were very diplomatic. Even when Gus and Tony were making fun of my suggestions, you handled them very well. You didn't shut any of us off. You kept all your avenues open. I admired that immediately in you. You have been trained very well in human behavior skills." I began to smile as he was talking when I remembered my father telling me on many occasions that I had no people skills. I just wish he were here at this table. I wondered if he'd agree with Dr. Elbie.

"The PRB is going to be a crucial part of the company in the next several months. Your participation is important. You will not be full time on the PRB but Calvin will. He will garner any resources needed to implement suggestions and you and he will push implementations through the system."

Dr. Elbie went on, "I think that this assignment can be fun and I hope that you elect to serve on the PRB team."

What can you say when bombarded like this? Of course I said yes. I was flattered, but concerned about having to work with Darth Vader.

We broke up for the evening and I was a member of the new PRB. I was not overly excited but at the same time I felt this was an important position. As Jim dropped me off, Dr. Elbie got into the front seat and they told me that we'd get together at 10:00 A.M. for the first meeting of the PRB.

As I came in the front door, Sandy was waiting anxiously. She had a look of anticipation. I had a smile so she knew everything was OK. She then relaxed. I told her about my new position and she was concerned about Darth Vader. We talked a little about what the new position would mean. I really didn't know. It would probably evolve, just as Dr. Elbie expected. It would continuously evolve into a useful part of the business or it would be disbanded.

We went to bed. I was exhausted and before I knew it, it was morning. Sandy was up with coffee as I came down for breakfast. The kids were still asleep. I sipped my coffee and gave Sandy a big hug as I headed out the door. I had a new bounce to my step. Quality Pump was going to make it and I had a chance to help insure its future.

Everyone had heard about the meeting at The Shanty.

Dr. Elbie arrived right on time and began the discussion. "I love the company rumor mill. As I was coming in, someone stopped me to ask if everything was OK. They apparently heard that there was a meeting last night at The Shanty. Let me say that you all still have jobs. The purpose of the meeting was to get agreement with Ed Daley of the union and *him,*" and Dr. Elbie pointed to me. "We are going to start a productivity review board, or PRB, to focus all ideas into action. We have had over four hundred ideas for wastes identified in the various classes over the last several weeks. Now we need a way to make sure that good ideas are acted upon in a timely manner."

He then paused and walked over in front of me, and just as he began to talk, Calvin came into the classroom and sat down. There was a gasp from one of the other guys who had recently joined Quality Pump from Osgood's. He didn't like Darth Vader either. You could hear him whisper, "It's Darth Vader!"

Dr. Elbie turned to the class and had Calvin stand up. Dr. Elbie introduced him as having joined Quality Pump from Osgood's. Mr. Grimes got up and came to the front of the room to take over for Dr. Elbie. He was all smiles because he really thought that Calvin was a fine addition to his staff. He was proud to have him for some reason. I wasn't so sure, but I was willing to wait and have him prove himself.

Calvin's sole job at Quality Pump was to manage the Productivity Review Board. He was to serve as support for any idea of waste elimination adopted by the PRB. He was to have no staff and was to use resources of those who would best be served by the idea.

Mr. Grimes sat down and Dr. Elbie introduced one of his associates, Dr. Mac Michels, who was to lead the class over the next week as it tried to define the role of the PRB more precisely. He was also going to work with the classes in defining the projects they wanted Mr. Grimes to support. In addition to all that, he was going to work with the managers and supervisers in defining their new roles in serving the various work teams.

Dr. Michels had known Dr. Elbie for a long time. He had a degree in industrial psychology and had worked as a machinist while he was in college. He seemed like a knowledgeable guy. He was a lot calmer than Dr. Elbie. He liked to use the flip charts instead of the board. He told us to call him Mac, and we did. As he began to talk about the PRB, Calvin asked, "I thought I was in charge of the PRB."

Everyone looked at Mr. Grimes. He turned to Calvin and said, "That's true, you are in charge of the PRB, but what the classes are going to do is define your job. You are serving the workers and the company, not the other way around. Your role is to do whatever it takes to make the defined objectives of the PRB work. I told you *that* in our interview and I made that clear in my offer letter to you." Mr. Grimes' voice suddenly got firm, "Calvin, do you have a problem with that? I thought we made all this clear last night and in all of our earlier discussions."

Calvin said, "I guess you are right. I just didn't think that my job would be open for public discussion, that's all. I didn't understand what Dr. Elbie was saying. You really are making this a total employee involvement organization. Believe me, Mr. Grimes, I don't have a problem with anything you said. I guess I was more surprised than anything. I didn't think you meant it when you said it. I like the idea of getting employees involved in implementing their ideas and redefining their work. If that's really what this is about, you have my total commitment to make it happen. I'm sorry for the confusion. I now see what you are doing. I like it and you have my support, my full support."

Mr. Grimes was glad to have Calvin on board, you could tell that. He then turned to the class, "And that goes for all of you. I want to turn this place around and I want all of you to continue to cooperate. It has been marvelous so far. I am anxious to see what else we can do. So give Calvin and the PRB your full support and lots of good things will happen."

16

Dr. Michels again addressed the class. He asked everyone again if they had any ideas about the PRB. After Mr. Grimes made his speech to Calvin and then to the class, it was clear that the PRB was important. Everyone was anxious to put in their ten cents. Buck jumped in first, "First of all, we have to make sure that we keep track of the number of steps we take off that Process Map. Remember that can put a few bucks in my pocket. Let's say that the first thing the PRB is responsible for is the Process Map. Every step eliminated is $1,000 for the kitty. If we divide it 120 ways that is $8.33 for me. So, as I said, that is number one priority for me."

Calvin couldn't follow the talk about the Process Map. He hadn't been in class during the discussion and he didn't know what the Process Map was. Dr. Michels pulled it out, unrolled the paper, and showed what the map looked like. Buck went up to the front of the class and explained it to Calvin and why it was so important to the PRB.

As soon as Buck finished his explanation, Calvin said, "OK, I understand. Every time we eliminate one of these lines, Mr. Grimes puts $1,000 in the kitty." He looked right at Mr. Grimes. "Did you agree to that?"

Mr. Grimes said he did, and he wanted to know the plan to be followed to insure that steps were eliminated. Calvin assured him that the PRB would manage that problem and report to him weekly. Calvin then asked the class, "Would you like the PRB to meet weekly?" Everyone nodded yes. "Where would you like me to post the minutes of our meetings and results of progress to date?"

No one had an idea. Mr. Grimes said, "I want to know what is going on and I want to know as it happens. As Dr. Elbie is fond of saying, we don't want to play a game and find the score out four weeks later. Let's post everything going on daily. Why don't we post everything on the bulletin board near the time clock? Everyone goes by there to get to the employee parking lot." When no one responded, he said, "OK, from now on, that is the PRB's exclusive board."

The bulletin board near the time clock was four feet high and twelve feet long. It had traditionally been reserved for union and safety business. Everyone agreed that it was a good spot to track PRB minutes and progress reports. It was a lot of space. Calvin gladly accepted the space for reporting the activities of the PRB.

Dr. Michels continued to probe for other ideas about responsibilities for the PRB. Gus was concerned about priorities. "How is Calvin going to set priorities? He hasn't been here long enough to know what is important. He might think he is doing a good job and he might be emphasizing the wrong things. I know it is important to have something like a PRB, but how do we handle these issues?"

As he looked at Dr. Michels for an answer, Dr. Michels came right back to the class, "Does anyone have any answers for Gus?"

Andrew raised his hand and Mac called on him. "You know, I've been thinking about this since the beginning. I now see how to prioritize the problems. That is very simple. We identify the wastes and we look at how big they are when we quantify them at $25 an hour. So that gives us a way to determine the size of the problems relative to each other. We can then estimate the costs to fix the waste. What do we do with this information? I can almost see what needs to be done but it isn't clear. Mac, do you have any way to organize the data so that Calvin and the PRB can make decisions we understand?"

"Bravo," Mac yelled. "Believe me, Andrew and I didn't team up and plan this but that was the perfect question to ask. Yes, as a matter of fact, we do have a technique that makes the process easy to follow. Here it is. First of all look in your workbooks and you will see the following chart."

FINANCIAL IMPACT SCREEN

	BENEFIT	
	LOW	HIGH
COST LOW	B TRIVIA	A PIECE OF CAKE
COST HIGH	D NO WAY	C MAYBE

He turned on the overhead projector and put on a transparency. "If you set your waste elimination size along the horizontal axis, you have what is called benefit. If you eliminate a waste, you are creating a benefit for the company. On this chart we equate benefit and waste. They are the same. One is the glass half full, a benefit, the other is a glass half empty, a waste. If you eliminate a waste you create a benefit for the company. Does everyone understand this?"

Tony was confused, "Is this what everyone else calls a cost-benefit analysis? I've seen them before but I never saw it presented this way. Why is this different?"

"Does anyone have any help for Tony?" Mac asked. "I do, but I would be interested in your input."

Jim was anxious to contribute and raised his hand. Mac acknowledged him and Jim responded, "I think that the way we did cost-benefit analysis before was always tied to buying a piece of equipment. We never seemed to do it for minor projects around the plant. We either did them or we didn't and we didn't have a way to easily prioritize some of the jobs. By expressing the waste eliminated as a benefit, everyone can see what is going on. Implementation decisions will be public knowledge; everyone can then understand what is happening. I like this because there are a lot of small projects that don't get done for any number of reasons.

"As I see the process, you identify the waste and cost it out. You then estimate the cost of fixing it or eliminating it. We have the PRB determine what we mean by high cost or low cost. We have Calvin and his team determine the point when the cost is a low cost or a high cost. So we look for those items that have low cost and high benefit. As I read the slide, you call that A Piece of Cake. Is that right?" Mac nodded and Jim continued, "When they are prioritized like this, they will get done if their cost is low and their benefit is high."

"Jim, that was excellent. Calvin, do you see why the PRB is so important?"

"Absolutely," Calvin answered. "Over the years, I have made a lot of decisions for all the wrong reasons. This approach won't keep us from making bad decisions but it will make it more difficult. We will be able to insure that identified wastes are eliminated and problems that are really screwing things up get taken care of quickly. I can see that, but I have another problem. How do we keep from making the following mistake? Suppose sales is getting ready to phase out a product line and we decide to fix a problem on that particular line, wouldn't we be wasting money? How do we prioritize that job? Doing it on a cost-benefit analysis alone won't tell me what to do."

Mac responded with a smile. You could tell that *Darth Vader* was smart. He might even be an OK guy. I liked the way he responded to Mr. Grimes and I really liked the problem he just identified. It even appeared that Calvin had anticipated Mac's next slide. As he put it up on the projector, Mac asked, "Can everybody see this?" Everyone nodded that they could.

MISSION RELEVANCE SCREEN

		MISSION RELEVANCE	
		LOW	HIGH
SUCCESS FACTOR	HIGH	GOOD FOR GROWTH C	STAR MATERIAL A
	LOW	BETTER GENERATE LOTS OF CASH D	GOOD FOR THE MASTER PLAN B

Mac went on, "See this slide? This completes the loop. If we know the project's relevance to the mission of the company and we know whether it is likely to be a successful project, we can fill in this chart. On one axis we have mission relevance. So we decide whether the project is of high or low relevance to the mission of the company."

At that point, Buck asked spontaneously, "What is the mission of this company?"

Mac turned to Mr. Grimes and asked him, "Do you have an answer?"

Mr. Grimes started to respond, but deferred to Roland. Roland was anxious to help at this point because Mr. Grimes was without a solid answer, "We don't call it a mission statement; we call it our goal. I don't have the business plan in front of me, but I think it reads something like: To become the best supplier of pumps in the industry."

Mac had a funny look on his face. His brows went up and he asked, "Is anyone familiar with the project to get someone to land on Mars?" Everyone nodded and Mac continued, "How would you describe the mission statement for that project?"

Mr. Grimes was interested in this issue and responded, "To land a man on Mars and return him to earth *alive.*" Everyone laughed at Mr. Grimes' humor and his emphasis.

"I would say that was a reasonably good answer in spite of the laughter," Mac noted. "And how would you relate that mission statement to the one Roland just gave? What should the mission statement contain? Is it the same as the goal or objective?"

Roland said, "I can't see the difference between a mission statement and a goal. Isn't our goal the same as a mission statement?"

"Well, to be quite frank, in my opinion, your statement was closer to a mission statement than a goal. I think of a mission statement as the overall reason why you are in business, and the goal is how you intend to achieve the mission. You may have a general mission and several goals that will allow you to complete the mission. Everyone in the company has the same mission but they may have different goals to contribute to the success of the mission.

"In your case, Roland, the sales department has a different set of goals than the production department. Each of your goals contributes to the success of the company mission. And your key results will measure the accomplishment of those things that need to be done to complete your goals. Is that clear?"

I was now starting to understand. We really needed a better mission statement than Roland gave moments earlier. We needed to restate the mission. I felt more comfortable with what was going on and so I jumped in with my thoughts. "Mac, if what you say is right, then we need to come up with a mission statement we can use for the PRB. Is that right?"

Mac nodded and I continued, "I would think we want to be the best pump manufacturer in the world that uses all employees to the max. Isn't that a possible mission statement?" Mr. Grimes agreed and I was now excited. "Isn't that what you and Dr. Elbie are preaching? You want everyone to contribute positively and you want us to be a good manufacturer. Excuse me, the best manufacturer. Right?"

Everyone was talking about my new mission statement and Buck was calling for a vote. "I like his statement. Let's say we vote on that as our new mission statement. It seems like a good one to start with. All those in favor."

"Hold it just a second, Buck," Mac exclaimed, "I think we need to have some more discussion before we take a vote. Does anyone else have anything to say?"

Bonnie had been quiet for several days but suddenly came to life,

"Mac, it seems to me that our company mission should talk about the quality of our product, the company's commitment to the environment and the community and a whole bunch of other things. To be the best pump manufacturer is just part of it."

Jim answered, "I agree with Bonnie. I think we need more in the mission statement. Can't we do all of that by saying we want to be a world class manufacturer. Doesn't that make sense?"

Mac answered, "It might if I knew what you meant by world class manufacturer. That expression or term has been bandied about quite a bit lately. I have my own understanding. What do you mean by that?"

Jim answered, "I think it is everything that Bonnie said. A world class manufacturer is a company that utilizes its people to the max, has high quality standards, uses JIT principles, is striving for continuous improvement of its operations and is concerned about the community and the environment. I think that just about covers it."

Mac complimented Jim and went on, "I like your definition. Are there other ideas, or are we ready to define the mission statement now?"

As the discussion continued, the following definitions evolved:

Mission Statement: To be the best world class manufacturer of pumps in the global market.
World Class Manufacturer: a company that
- utilizes its people to the max,
- has high quality standards,
- uses JIT principles,
- is striving for continuous improvement of its operations,
- and is concerned about the community and the environment.

Mac turned to the class and asked, "Is this your definition?"

Everyone looked around the room and generally agreed. Buck said again, "I move that we vote on this definition." Everyone voted for it, even Roland and Mr. Grimes.

Mac then said, "I think we have enough to continue on with the slide." He turned back to the overhead projector. "Given the definition of the mission statement, how would we handle the situation that Calvin brought up? How would we deal with a product line that was being discontinued?"

Tony said, "That's really easy, isn't it? If we aren't going to be making it any more, then it has nothing to do with our mission. It isn't going to get us to Mars. Right? We aren't going to be selling any more of them so the PRB has an easy decision. They don't do it because it isn't part of our selling strategy. If we don't sell any, we shouldn't make any. And the success criteria issue isn't even a concern. We only want to make those items that are high in relevance to the mission and are high in the success criteria. This is easy. It makes sense."

"Thank you very much, Tony," Mac responded. "I'm glad you understand this. Does anyone not understand what we are talking about here?" No one raised their hand. Mac asked another question, "OK, let's see how much you really understand. Suppose that you have the following situation."

One of the workers on the shop floor comes up with a way to cut lead time by 80% on a product that accounts for 20% of your current business. You are intending to phase the product out of the product line next year with a radical new product. The worker's solution is simple. It involves moving equipment needed to manufacture the product into one area of the factory. The total cost of all the new jigs and fixtures and the cost of the move is no more than $1,500. What does Calvin's group do?

Everyone was silent for a moment. Calvin asked if he could answer. Mac nodded affirmatively. So Calvin said, "That is pretty straightforward, if I understand what you are doing. First, this is very easy to do, so the cost would be low. The waste eliminated would be significant. If you could deliver the product in three weeks instead of twelve, your customers would be very happy. You might even be able to gain market share. If the product stays in the factory less time, you will have less work in process, so your inventory will go down. If this product accounts for 20% of the revenues and you can cut its contribution to the inventory by 75%, then you are going to reduce the inventory by 15%.

"If you just keep the product going for two more years, you will add an additional one million dollars a year to the bottom line. And although its mission relevance is low—you are phasing the product out—it has a very high success criteria. I would recommend doing it in a minute." He hesitated. "Yeah, I know what's missing from our definition of mission and a world class manufacturer. You know what we forgot? We forgot to put in anything about making money. If we change the definition of a world class manufacturer, we should change the first line of the definition to read: A *profitable* manufacturing company that . . . With that change it reads like this," and Calvin went up to the board and made the correction so that the definition now read:

World Class Manufacturer: a profitable manufacturing company that
- utilizes its people to the max,
- has high quality standards,
- uses JIT principles,
- is striving for continuous improvement of its operations,
- and is concerned about the community and the environment.

"And with this change in the definition, I think we have a fine mission statement. Have I answered your earlier question?"

I didn't follow his logic. He went too fast. I understood what he said about the definition, but I didn't understand the other stuff. Mac asked Calvin to slow down and go over the numbers more slowly. He obliged and most of us got it the second time. Boy, was he smart. He was also very good at explaining things and took special care to insure that we all understood. Maybe he was going to be alright, but I still had my reservations.

Mac thought that was enough for the day and dismissed us a few minutes early. He asked Calvin and me to stay around after class and we obliged. Mac was all business. He wanted to get going. After everyone was out of the room, he said, "Why don't we spend a few minutes trying to establish an agenda for your 10:00 A.M. meeting?" We agreed. "I would say rule number one in any project like this is to always start meetings with an agenda, a typewritten agenda. And, in my experience, rule number two is to end the meeting in one hour. You are wasting time after one hour. Break up the meeting into two meetings of one hour each if you need to meet for two hours. That way everybody gets there on time. As Dr. Elbie likes to do, post the minutes of every meeting and include the number of minutes that anyone is late. Late minutes add up. Let everyone know that you intend to post the number of minutes that anyone is late, and before long, no one will be late. Your meetings will start on time and you will get a lot more accomplished."

We defined the agenda for the ten o'clock meeting. Mr. Grimes, Bonnie from sales, Jim, Al (the shop chief steward), Calvin and I were all to be in attendance. Al had been one of Jack's boys and was slow in coming around to the ideas that Mac and Dr. Elbie were preaching. He had a problem with the idea of measuring people. When Mac and Dr. Elbie talked about work as involving planning, controlling and doing, he got nervous. He had never been measured, nor seen a measurement that was not used to fire someone.

The PRB meeting started right on schedule. Mac was teaching the third class and Dr. Elbie came in to substitute for Mac while he attended the PRB meeting. We were in the conference room and Calvin called the meeting to order. Al agreed to take the minutes and to post them before quitting time. This was intended to give all the employees a chance to see what happened at the meeting.

Calvin ran the meeting efficiently. We decided to post the definitions of mission statement and world class manufacturer on the PRB bulletin board and get input either in class or from people directly. We spent time defining the goals of the PRB and decided that these might be a good start.

The PRB has the following goals and measurements of success:

1. To monitor the organization's efficiency of processing orders compared to the Process Map developed in Class 1. Every step eliminated from the total of 61 will be documented by the PRB and submitted to Mr. Grimes on the last day of each month. Each step eliminated will generate $1,000 for the kitty and will be distributed quarterly to the employees.

2. To receive ideas from employees that recommend elimination of waste. For every idea of waste elimination of $25,000 or less that is implemented, an employee will be paid a bonus of $25. For wastes greater than $25,000 but less than $100,000, a bonus of $50 will be paid. For anything over $100,000 of waste identified and the program for elimination initiated, a minimum bonus of $100 will be paid with a negotiated bonus for really big wastes. Any idea submitted by one of the established teams will receive triple the bonus noted, with proceeds distributed equally to all team members. The reason for the

bonus for team ideas is that some ideas are a group effort and no one person should receive the full credit.

a. All ideas should be submitted on the attached cards, distributed around the shop and available from any member of the PRB.

b. All action on ideas will be responded to weekly with the results of successes posted for all to see. Total accumulated wastes eliminated to date and total payouts will be posted weekly. A report will post: ideas pending, ideas approved but not completed, ideas implemented and bonus paid.

c. There will be situations that arise where an idea will be submitted and the committee thinks it is too close to the normal definition of a job. For instance, if an engineer comes up with the design for a new valve, it will probably not receive an idea award because that is his job. If a machinist comes up with a design, he will be rewarded. The PRB reserves the right to make judgments when there is some question as to the merit of the idea.

3. The chairman of the PRB will be supportive of any implementation of an approved idea. He will commandeer any and all resources needed to get the job completed. The chairman will report directly to Mr. Grimes.

This declaration was signed by everyone who attended the meeting. Calvin brought the completed minutes around for me to see in the early afternoon. They were posted by quitting time. In class, Mac had forgotten about the PRB. It was functioning well. By the end of the first week we had twenty-three ideas to review. Calvin was busy. Mac called a lunch meeting of the managers and supervisers to go over a few items of concern that he had heard about.

Mac was explaining that teams were going to pull some power and control away from the supervisers and managers. It was only logical. He was just pointing out his opinion about why most Quality Circles fail. "Now, let me ask you this. In the process that Dr. Elbie has been discussing, what is the definition of work?"

One of the supervisers answered, "Work is planning, controlling and doing."

"OK, now," Mac went on, "if workers were only doing before, and now they are controlling and planning their work, where did these functions come from?"

"From us," everybody responded.

"Good." Mac was showing some enthusiasm, "And now what does this mean for the whole organization?"

Someone shouted, "The whole damn organization is going to change."

"And where does that lead?"

"To a new culture and way of working."

"Does everybody see what is happening and why it is happening?" We all nodded that we understood. Mac went on, "One of the areas of specialty that I have worked on over the years is creating culture change in organizations. And my studies have shown that a successful change occurs when three things are present, whether we are talking about individual, group, or system change." He went to the flip chart and wrote the following:

Three Things Needed for Successful Change

1. Ability to Change
2. Willingness to Change
3. System to Support the Change.

"What does this mean?"

Jim said, "It means that in order to change, a company or a person or even a group of people must have a basic ability to change. They must have the skills needed to make the change occur. To do this we normally train, to provide the knowledge, skills and capabilities to insure that the change can occur. If someone doesn't have the required skills, you can't expect them to change to some new environment. It is the manager's job to make sure that those skills are there.

"As for willingness, they must also be willing to change. They must be willing to apply their skills to cause the change to occur. Mac, I'm not so sure whether willingness or ability comes first. It almost appears to be a chicken and egg situation."

Mac responded, "I like your response so far. And yes, there is a chicken and egg situation here. If you have the ability to change, namely, you know what to do, it's easy to proceed. If peer pressure keeps you from implementing the change, you clearly don't have the willingness.

"Let me give you an example that I find humorous. When I was in college I worked one summer on a ranch in Wyoming. Of all things,

The New Turnaround

an OSHA inspector arrived at the ranch and decided that cowboy hats were not sufficiently safe to protect cowboys in their ranch duties. From his view, every cowboy needed to wear a hard hat. So that change was ordered.

"Clearly, the cowboys understood all the reasons for his analysis, but they didn't want to change. They liked their cowboy hats. Needless to say, the cowboy hats stayed, but the OSHA inspector was unceremoniously removed from the premises, physically.

"I use that example because it represents a group of workers who have the ability but not the willingness to change.

"Let's talk about Quality Pump. Many people have told Dr. Elbie and me that they really think that change is necessary. They have the willingness to change, but they lack the skills. They do not have the ability. So they need to be trained.

"Jim, you are right; it is almost a chicken and egg situation, but it is more. More than ability and willingness needs to be present for any change to last. Jim, could you continue with your explanation?"

Jim went on, "And I think by system you must mean those things that are needed to support the change. What you are saying by system, I guess, is all those things that make the change stick. If you don't put a system of support in place then the change will only last for a little while."

Mac went on, "Jim, that's right about the system. Who controls the system?"

Calvin was quiet during most of the discussion and finally answered, "All of us in this room and any of the other managers not in attendance at this meeting. The managers control the system, right?"

"You've got it, Calvin, I think you've got it!" Mac was pleased that the discussion was going so well. You could see it on his face. "And what are the support systems that we are talking about here?"

Jerry, a shift superviser from the maintenance department, who had missed quite a few of his classes because of machine failures and other breakdowns, blurted out, "I think this is just crap. I don't understand a thing you are saying."

Mac looked at Jerry and asked, "What don't you understand?"

"I don't understand why we are talking about change. Since you've been saying that everything we do is so bad, why don't we just close the doors and be done with it? I think everything that's going on here is stealing money from our bonuses. That's what I think. This company is in big trouble, and this program isn't going to fix it. Let's just struggle the way we've been for another couple of years and then I can retire."

"So you want to leave everything the way it is just so that you can retire in peace?" Mac asked.

Jerry replied sarcastically, "Yep, that's about it! I think that Dr. Elbie sure talks a big game. I don't think you guys can deliver for us. And it seems like nothing but busy work."

"Why do you think Dr. Elbie and I are going to do anything? We told you right up front that we don't make the changes, you do. To be honest, Jerry, I think what you are suggesting is selfish. You have only a couple of years left and there are a number of people in this room who want to be working here in twenty years so that they can also retire."

Mac got a bit heated. "I think *that* is what is wrong with America. Everyone is watching out for themselves and not thinking about anyone else. You can't get by with that attitude anymore. It's that kind of thinking that gets us into wars, that causes mergers to put people out of work, that creates homelessness in the cities and then doesn't do anything about it. It's selfish. I won't let that go by for one minute. We can't just think about today. We have to pull together as a large team to make sure that we pay attention to the stakes of everyone, today and in the future.

"Dr. Elbie and I wouldn't be working with you if we thought you were failures and couldn't get the job done. *We won't do the work.* You will. And you will be proud of the company you create. It will be healthy financially and it will be a fun place to work. In order to get there, you do have to change and that is what started this discussion.

"Jerry, forgive me for getting upset, but I meant everything I said. And you are entitled to your opinion, even if I disagree with you. I think you can make your retirement a happy one if you know, Jerry, that you helped make the company healthy. You helped *change* to a better way of working. And maybe you can even lead the way.

"Don't give me any crap about only a short time until retirement. Think of the past, and of all the things you have wanted to change in the way the company was managed. You now have a chance to do something about that and make it right for those who follow you."

While Mac was cranking, everyone was silent. Everyone was paying attention. Earlier, he had appeared to be a pretty mellow guy and didn't appear to be bothered by negative people like Jerry. After his speech everyone stood up and clapped. Even Jerry managed a few

The New Turnaround

claps. Order settled back and Jerry responded, "I guess I hit one of your buttons, didn't I?" Everyone laughed at Jerry's attempt at a peace offering.

"I really am sorry, Mac. I wasn't trying to be just selfish and negative. I was trying to understand why we even need to worry about these issues of change. You and Dr. Elbie are trying to make rocket scientists out of us, and all we want to do is row a boat. You two guys are doing a great job; just tell us where to aim and we'll do it."

Mac smiled when Jerry finished. He looked out the window of the door as if to collect his thoughts. He turned and spoke directly to Jerry. "You know, Jerry, I really don't know the best way to respond to your statement. I could be angry but I'm not. I could feel encouraged but again, I'm not. I guess I'm just *whelmed.*"

Everyone sort of smiled at his humor and Mac went on. "Jerry, the only reason we explain any of this stuff to you or anyone is so that you can understand why we are doing what we are doing. It isn't a precise science. Nothing involving human beings is. We think we have some ideas that might, and I reemphasize the word *might,* help you and the company get to a state of profitability faster. That's the only reason we are allowed to do what we do. We have found a better way to organize companies that helps them operate more profitably. And you know what else?" Mac paused. "It will be more fun to work at the resulting company.

"Let me ask you one more question, OK?" Jerry nodded his acceptance. "Jerry, would you really rather work in the company as it existed before or as we say it should be after the training is over?"

"I really can't answer that. I sort of see where you are going, but for some reason I can't envision working in that environment. It's taken me over thirty years to figure this company out as it was a month ago, and I don't have thirty more years to figure out this new one. But I do accept the fact that some of these younger people may work here thirty years and I should help them create a company that survives that long. So, I will cooperate and I will support your efforts.

"You must understand that Mr. Grimes is pretty hardnosed about certain things. For some reason, he has been going along with this process. And I don't think you've crossed him yet. When you do cross him and survive, I think all of us will feel more confident that you may have something.

"Look, Mac, this is pretty basic. If you make Grimes angry and he chases you guys out the door, what do we do? We look to you for support, all of us do. If you get your asses thrown out, we still have to deal with him. He has a temper and he's going to come after those of us who turned on him. He's done that in the past. I'm sorry to say that, but that's how I feel. I've been through a lot and I just want to make it through the next twenty-one months."

Mac was speechless for a moment. Jerry really had a handle on the problem, but Mac wanted to proceed. "Jerry, you have made a good point. If Mr. Grimes wants to throw us out because he gets pissed at us, then you people suffer. We lose a contract and some momentary cash flow, but you have an angry Mr. Grimes to deal with. I understand that.

"I think that is the reason we have been successful wherever we have worked. The owner knows that he has to do something and he does it. He hires us and then has to eat crow." Everyone chuckled and relaxed a bit as Mac's calm demeanor and speech soothed our anxieties. "Mr. Grimes has had to eat a lot of crow so far. I can't tell you how many times Mr. Grimes has eaten crow already. He hasn't liked crow one bit. And you know what, Jerry, we still haven't provided any catsup. He's eaten every crow, feathers and all, without catsup." Again, everyone was smiling at Mac's humor.

"Let me give you an example. Did Mike Cain start his employment here before you?" Jerry nodded. "Do you think that it was easy for Mr. Grimes to terminate Mike? I don't think it was. Mike was a longtime employee, but Mike was sabotaging this process. On top of it, he endangered the life of one of the employees. And Mike didn't show any concern for him. For Mr. Grimes to do what he had to do was a tough job. He did it because he's committed. He sees what this process can accomplish and he didn't want anyone getting in the way. Not even Mike. So he encouraged Mike's resignation. Believe me, that was very painful for Mr. Grimes. Every time he eats another crow, he gets further committed to the process. He's almost there and I think he will be there and firmly committed when he starts to see the results on the bottom line. That's what this program is all about.

"I've talked a lot today, and I want to continue this discussion. When we do, we'll talk about what we mean by the system." As I clocked out for the day, I realized that I had to go to a parents club meeting with Sandy. I hated these meetings because they really dragged on.

As Sandy and I got into the car to head over to the school, I looked up, and the baby-sitter was holding the baby at the window and he was waving at us. Sandy and I waved back as I pulled the car out of the driveway. I was actually relaxed as we headed into town. The meeting started and a number of issues were raised. The meeting was running smoothly until we hit the big issue of the evening, the decision to build the playground structure. The discussion had been going on for over forty-five minutes when I raised my hand. Sandy almost dropped dead in her seat. I had never spoken at any meeting, let alone a parents meeting, which were never interesting, and I had never felt that I could contribute. They were talking about spending $40,000 to put an elaborate playground structure in place. One of the alternatives that no one had considered was spending 20%, or $8,000, and taking care of 80% of our children's immediate needs. I offered that suggestion and everyone agreed to spend $8,000 of our treasury to test the initial part of the structure and add the rest if the children used it.

That made sense to everyone. On the way home Sandy was pleased to hear me sound so intelligent. I told her that it was what I had learned at work.

17

In class the next morning we got into a discussion of the causes of some of the wastes; it got pretty exciting. Dr. Elbie and Mac were directing the discussion around the inventory control problem that had been identified earlier as a five million dollar waste.

The issue turned to the *point of control*. Dr. Elbie was explaining and Delmer, one of the MRP production control supervisors, began to argue with him. "I don't care what you say, Dr. Elbie, the storeroom has to control what goes on in the shop. We must be able to know when all jobs are running and be able to schedule the materials for each job for each machine. That way we can know what's going on and control the jobs. Right now, no one knows what's going on out there. We should be the point of control. Certainly, you don't expect *them* to be the point of control."

Dr. Elbie answered, "The only thing that I expect out of you and this company is that you will organize the business to minimize waste and maximize profits. There are three problems associated with the point of control. One of them is *multiple* points of control. That happens when an event or an action can be started by more than one person. We have already seen many examples of that, haven't we Tony?" Tony and Gus were sitting next to each other and they managed to laugh about the situation. "The second problem is the *wrong* point of control. The last problem is *no* point of control.

"A wrong point of control, occurs when the control is activated by the wrong person or department. We have already discussed why storerooms are a waste. They don't add value. In my definition of a waste, we want to get rid of them, don't we? So why would you want the storeroom to control anything? Especially if you want to get rid of it. All I am saying is that the storeroom is the wrong point of control. The point of control should be the shop. Does everyone see that?"

Delmer got defensive. "You mean to tell me that my job of managing the storeroom is a waste? That there shouldn't be a storeroom?"

Dr. Elbie answered, "Right, and where should the storeroom be?"

Jim jumped in, "Are you telling us that we should build a storeroom out on the shop floor? That would be a bigger waste of money."

"No, not really. I am saying that you shouldn't have any storeroom, any inventory, at all. Inventory is a waste. It should be eliminated completely. You should put the burden on your suppliers in exchange for some guarantees. You should strengthen your relationship with your suppliers. We will talk about this later. Believe me, it can be done, but I'm sure you can find reasons why it won't work here!"

Delmer got back into it. "Dr. Elbie, I think you are insulting us. We do a good job in the storeroom and you are saying that we are a waste."

"First of all, Delmer, I know you are doing a good job. The question I come back to all the time is this: are you doing the right work? Delmer, we did a Process Map of the flow of an order into the shop from the sales department. Over 60% of the steps from the arrival of an order to the shop until a job was completed involved material tracking operations. To my way of thinking, that is excessive. We costed the number of minutes to process the material tracking operations and it was at least 30 hours per day for everyone in the operation. That amounts to a waste of $750 per day or $187,500 of waste per year just to track orders. That is amazing. Why should you do that?"

Delmer was getting more defensive. "Because that is the way our computer system or our MRP system tracks jobs. You have to understand that an MRP system is a very sophisticated piece of software. If those steps are there, they are there for auditing reasons and for a whole host of other reasons. They are all needed. Believe me, they are needed."

Dr. Elbie wasn't going to let Delmer off the hook. He bored right in with his questioning. "Delmer, could you get me a routing sheet for the product that accounts for most of your business? If you go get that routing sheet then maybe you can explain some things to me."

Delmer said that he didn't know which one to get. Mr. Grimes told him that the 255 MT was the biggest mover and so Delmer headed out the door. While he was gone, Dr. Elbie explained the kanban concept of controlling product flow on the shop floor and in assembly. He explained to us that *kanban* means "to signal" in Japanese.

Kanban was a signal to order a batch of widgets, to make a batch of grommets, or to fill an empty kanban box with nuts or bolts. It was a signal that contained key information about the part. If a series of parts was required to fill the empty box, the kanban order would tell the machinist where the drawings were.

He explained that one of the ways to use an MRP system and a kanban system was in fact pretty clever. Mac explained that most MRP systems identify a primary and secondary location for each part. Some even allow four or more locations for every part. "And it turns out that your MRP system has that capability. We have used it at other shops."

At that moment Delmer came back and with him was John Alphonse, the data processing manager, and another guy I didn't recognize. John introduced the other guy as his computer sales representative. He wanted to sit in on this discussion and asked Mac and Dr. Elbie if it was OK. They didn't mind.

The fireworks then started. Delmer gave Mac and Dr. Elbie each copies of the routing sheet for the 255 MT. Mac looked at it a minute and Dr. Elbie went down the hall to make a transparency. He came back quickly and gave the overhead to Mac, who put it on the overhead projector and began, "Ah, here it is. Just like we thought. Let's look at the beginning of the routing sheet for a moment. In the MRP system, you start with the following sequence:

1. move from the storeroom to the first operation—day of operation
2. wait for the machine's availability—per schedule
3. setup the machine—1 hour
4. run the parts—16 hours and 54 minutes
5. move to storage area for subassemblies.

"You heard Dr. Elbie and me saying that we were expecting to find something here. And we did."

At this point John Alphonse took over for Delmer. John was going to defend this document. "The reason I came in here is that I heard about what you did over at Prescott's to the MRP system. And you are not going to do that here. I have one of the better shops around the area and I feel we can change other things but we can't mess with the MRP system and the materials flow that we have established. This is my territory and you aren't going to do to me what you did to Peter Schmit at Prescott's."

Mac looked at Dr. Elbie and they both had puzzled looks on their faces. Mac asked John, "Would you please tell me what we did to Peter? I talked with him two weeks ago and he seemed pretty happy. What did we do to him that was so bad? He has a slightly different position than the one he had before. I thought he liked his new job. Maybe you know something that we don't."

The New Turnaround

John went on, "I talked with Peter about six months ago and he was ready to kill both of you guys for messing with his operation. He had one of the better MRP shops around. I know what you did." John almost sounded deranged.

Mac was trying to be gentle, but John interrupted him as he started to speak, "I'm telling you, don't mess with my operation!"

At that point, Mr. Grimes got into the discussion. "John, I don't like your attitude. I thought you were a professional. You may not like things that are being suggested about changes that need to be made. Some of the changes may effect your organization, but don't let me hear you say anything like that again. Everything is up for change. Even your department." Someone in the background mumbled, "maybe even your job."

Mr. Grimes stood up and the computer account rep moved his chair away from John Alphonse. You could tell, when the blood was going to be spilled, that he was not going to be bloodied.

"And furthermore, why did you come into this class? Your class is right after lunch."

John answered sheepishly, "Delmer needed my help and I offered to come in to help him in this discussion."

Mr. Grimes responded boldly, "I was very impressed by Delmer. He seemed to be holding his own, though he seems very defensive about the MRP system. As Dr. Elbie has shown me over the last several weeks, I should be suspect whenever I see that. Why are you and Delmer so defensive? Are you hiding something?"

John immediately stood his ground, "We aren't hiding anything. We just don't think that the MRP system should be changed. We've worked so hard to make it right. We can now do scheduling every week right on target. We get all our reports to you on time and we have an accurate tracking on our inventory. Dr. Elbie and Mac here are trying to change all that. I'm just protecting the system that all the people in my department have worked so hard to create. It works. Why fool with it?"

I had been looking at the overhead during all this discussion and I suddenly saw what Dr. Elbie and Mac had been looking for. It was right there. So I jumped in, "I beg to differ with you, John."

Everyone turned to look in my direction. It was a good feeling. I knew what to say and I did. "As I see it, *your* system does not work. And I think I see why. Look at the information up on the board. It shows a 1 hour setup. I set up that job two days ago and it took 6 hours and 35 minutes. *Not 1 hour.* And the run time was not 16 hours and 54 minutes. It currently has been running for 22 hours and is still 5 hours from completion. It would appear to me that if you are going to brag about your system, you'd better make sure you don't have a lot of garbage in it."

Tony and Gus both said simultaneously, "Right on, my man, right on!"

So I continued, "I think you have bad figures and your schedules are always wrong. Overtime is a waste. If we follow your schedule, we are always going to have to work overtime. That is not an efficient way to run any shop. If I have learned anything as a machinist and as a manager and from this class, it is that. I think if we managed the shop with your schedule, Quality Pump would be broke in a month. Your system may work in your office but it certainly doesn't help us run the shop.

"I think if we work together, we can find a way to use your system, but believe me, right now it doesn't help us run anything. You don't have to be defensive, John, we don't hate you. We just think that the system that you think is great, *isn't*. It isn't your fault. *We are not blaming you.* Just make it work in a way that will help us get the work out. We know you can do it, we just don't think we need to worship your fine work. Give us information that helps us."

Mac looked at me and said, "That was very good. I see you are catching on."

Mr. Grimes was acting as if he had to go. He jumped up and asked if he could face the class. Mac walked away from the front of the class and gave Mr. Grimes a lot of room. This discussion had gotten him agitated and everyone could see that what he was about to say was very serious. "You know ladies and gentlemen, I don't think everyone understands that I am serious when I say, I want this business to get fixed. If the systems aren't working, fix them."

He looked straight at John, "If you generate data that nobody uses, stop generating it. As Jack Elbie says, that's a waste. If everyone pulls together, we can make this business work. John, you must support these people on the floor, not control them. Yours is a service organization. So start acting like it and give these people what they want. Do you understand that?"

John said "Yes, Mr. Grimes, I understand."

"If I hear of any resistance from you or any of your people, then you are going to hear from me full blast. John, I want this process to work. I almost feel like I'm preaching something that I read on someone's desk here, the beatings will continue until morale picks up. I do want good morale here, but we need everyone to cooperate to achieve our goal of profitability in the next quarter. Does everyone understand?"

Everyone nodded and Mr. Grimes sat down. Mac came to the front again and looked at me and said, "You were trying to say something a moment ago."

"Yeah, I've been thinking about this for a few days. I think that the 255 MT could be manufactured a lot differently. We are learning lots of new things in this class and we have one project that Tony and I are working on that is going to be terrific when we make our presentation to Mr. Grimes.

"Mac, I would like to get something off my chest. I have just joined this company from Osgood's. I got laid off when the plant closed down. I recently lost a good friend who was depressed over the plant closure and killed himself when he was drunk. He ran into a tree. John, I don't give a shit about your goddamn computer unless it can help us get the work out, unless it helps speed the process of adding value.

"I do see where they are leading us in this class. And I think I want to work at that company. I'm excited about what's going on. Maybe the 255 MT could be . . . ," I hesitated a moment.

Mac then jumped in, "Those are very good points and I recall reading about your friend's death. I was sorry to hear about that." Mac waited a second before continuing. "If I do say so, I think you people have earned your money today. Tomorrow we are going to get into lead time and the effect that it has in creating wastes. Maybe we can look at the 255 MT tomorrow as the basis of the discussion. Have a good day and we'll see you tomorrow."

Everyone got up to leave and Mr. Grimes came over to me. He said good-bye to everybody and after the room cleared out, he said "I was really proud of what you said in class today. I like your contribution and I am looking forward to the presentation from you, Tony and the crew." He really made me feel good.

I went back out to the floor and Calvin was waiting for me at my work center. He had a big smile on his face as I approached. He said, "I just wanted to say that you spoke very well in the class. I think you understand more of what Mac and Dr. Elbie are saying than I do. I was intrigued by your ideas about the 255 MT. Could I buy you lunch today?"

As he said that, I corrected him, "Don't yuppies usually say, could we *do* lunch today?" We laughed. I started to say yes but then I remembered, "No, Calvin, I can't. Mac is going to give us a little more stuff on the systems support part of change. I don't really want to miss that. Don't you have to be there?"

Calvin looked shocked. "You know, I completely forgot. I never do that. Guess that's a sign of old age." Again, we both laughed.

As Calvin went away, he waved and said, "See you in the den!"

I guess he meant den of iniquities. Because that's what it was becoming. Most of the supervisers were really afraid that they were going to lose their jobs if we got too productive. They could see what was happening. Everyone in the company was catching on. Workers were going to have more control of their jobs. The planning and control functions of the work were going to be taken from the supervisers and managers. And that we understood, but we didn't expect it to happen so fast. It was happening.

Lunchtime arrived and I headed up to the conference room. Here I was going into a meeting with Calvin, aka, *Darth Vader. Darth Vader,* the man who closed Osgood's, was now my compadre. He attended classes with me as a fellow student. And he didn't know any more about any of this than I did. In fact, he was now in my territory. If anything, I could help him understand some of the stuff.

Mac came in. Dr. Elbie was wrapping up another class and Phil was working with one of the teams on the setup issue. Things were moving right along. As Mac called the meeting to order, he asked the group a question, "Do you people think that Dr. Elbie, Phil and I could first of all teach you to understand all about VAP and then have you, instead of us, go teach or facilitate the process? Do you think that would be a more or less efficient way to do this training?"

Jim smiled and got right into it. "Oh, I see what you are doing. You and Dr. Elbie are trying to justify your consulting fees and now you are trying to convince us. Right?"

Mac also smiled in his response. "Yes, in a way, I am justifying our approach. I believe it is the right way to start this process in a company, but I am interested in your opinions. Why should or shouldn't you guys and gals first be trained and then teach the others? I think that is a fair question to ask."

Calvin liked these kinds of questions. His hand went up as his signal of readiness and he began, "I have participated in Train the Trainer programs at General Motors. They seemed to work quite well in a lot of programs. I think they work well when you are just training something like math or programming or something that is a specific skill.

"*There is something different about this training.* I can almost see it but . . . ," he hesitated a minute and excitedly he continued, "Yeah, I see what it is. This training is messing with the organization, the work, the jobs of everyone. If we were first instructed to learn the process and then transfer it to all the workers, we would probably be in the way. Because our jobs would be affected.

"I remember that Dr. Elbie called it, *the fox watching the hen house.* If our jobs are going to change, we would not be as willing to encourage the process and it would probably go much slower. Is that what you were looking for?"

"Yes, Calvin, that's exactly what I was looking for. And your explanation was quite succinct. I liked it." As I listened to Calvin, I could understand everything he was saying. I really understood what Mac and Dr. Elbie were trying to do here. At first, training us didn't make sense. You have to train everybody in the company at the same time. *That's the key.* Then, any new people can be trained by members of their team. By jove, I think I've got it.

Chris Sneider, the head of accounting, was really against any training that made his people more knowledgeable about what went on in the company. All the people in his department had complained that he tried to keep information from them. For Chris, knowledge was power. And boy did he love that power.

As Mac finished speaking, Chris asked if he could say something. Mac acknowledged his request. By his body language you could tell that Chris was ready to argue. "Look, I have worked other places and I have been trained to be a good manager. I think that I have a lot of integrity and could teach the people in my group to do this stuff."

At this point, he was interrupted by Calvin, "Don't you see Chris, Mac isn't saying that we would be training just the people in our own department, we would be training the people in other departments as well. It would be just like the VAP training. You would have people from the shop floor, from engineering, from the dock, from all over the company. Mac is saying that the training of all workers together allows us to go back to the basic questions, **What is the work that adds value?** and **Are we doing the right work now to get that value-added** *job completed?* And we aren't the people who can ask that impartially."

Chris countered, "I think I am a fair and impartial person and that training me would be a good idea. I certainly can do what Mac and Dr. Elbie are doing."

Jim was interested in this issue, and asked to be recognized. "OK, Chris, I know you are a fair person. Suppose you are doing a session with the workers and they come up with a suggestion that might change *your* job. What is really going to happen?"

Chris was ready for the challenge and answered, "I feel I am a professional and would be able to handle the situation. If my job was totally eliminated because it was determined to be a total waste, then I would accept that. I would try to find a job that was not a waste and see if Mr. Grimes would give me the opportunity to do the new job. I really don't see the problem."

Jim shook his head and Mac asked matter of factly, "Chris, I'm impressed by your commitment to this process. How many of your buddies in this class would be so generous? Would anyone else be able to lead a class that proposed the elimination of his or her job? Let's have a show of hands." None went up except for Chris's.

Mac went on, "Does anyone else have any input on this issue?"

No one did, so Chris continued, "I think this whole discussion is bullshit. No one is going to eliminate my job, but that wouldn't be a problem for me even if it did happen. I can see that some of the others may have a problem. We are mandated by law on how we keep our records and report our information to the IRS and the state. We really aren't subject to any of the problems everyone else has. That's why I like accounting. Everything is precise. Managing is very easy. There is no room for deviation from the standards."

No one in the room could believe Chris. Was he crazy? Of course he has standards to adhere to, we all did, but if he thought he couldn't make things better, then maybe he was a big problem. Why would he say such a thing in front of all of us? It was suicide to say such a thing even in a *No Blame* environment. Everyone was confused about his motive.

Chris went on, "I don't think there are many things that we need to do differently. It's OK for everyone else, but we have our house in order. Believe me, we have our house in order."

Mac was smiling and started to roll up his sleeves, "Chris, I am impressed by what you are saying. It is very difficult to run any department, let alone the accounting department, with any amount of control and competence. I've heard from everyone in the organization that you run a tight ship."

Chris acknowledged the kudos with great relish. He was basking in the momentary recognition of his talents. He was good, but I could see the punch coming. Mac went on, "Chris, do you think you have a good handle on the various numbers?"

"Yes, I do. We can tell you any number you need. Just ask."

Mac went on, "Don't worry, Chris, I will. I will."

At that moment, John Alphonse apologized for coming in late. It was evident he was still smarting from his morning session. As he sat down, Mac was just getting ready to ask his question, "And so, Chris, what is the most important number that is tracked by the accounting department?"

Chris was ready for this one. "That's easy! *The profits.*"

Mac looked at Chris and thought a minute. Someone to my right said, "No, it isn't. We need to know how long it takes to get a goddamn new product to market. Tracking the profits is easy. Tracking the time to get a product to market will allow us to survive."

I tried to look down the conference table to see who was speaking, and it was Andrew, the engineer. He was really getting into the training and had a new insight here. Mac was almost surprised by the answer. "Andrew, how did you arrive at that? That is exactly where I was trying to lead the group. Did someone tell you that? I'm amazed. No one ever comes to that conclusion. What made you?"

Andrew was proud of himself. "Dr. Elbie told this to Mr. Grimes before the training began. I overheard the discussion. I was out in the shop for some reason and was standing by the two of them when they were talking. It didn't make sense at the time but as the training was going on, I began to think about it. Now it really makes sense. You need to track profits but you also need to track your system's ability to respond to new ideas. That is a very interesting way to measure how everyone is performing as a team."

Andrew really amazed me. I had never gotten to know him prior to the training and I probably never would have if it weren't for the class contact.

Anyway, Chris was not impressed. "That doesn't tell Mr. Grimes anything about how he is doing. Measuring the revenue and the expenses does. Everyone knows that. That, my friend, is not rocket science. That's business 101!"

"You're right, Chris, that is business 101," said Mac. "What I am saying is that they don't need to pay you a fancy salary to do that. Any of your assistants could give Mr. Grimes those numbers. What you really need to be doing is looking at better ways to measure the financial position of the company and to know that you are reporting the true and important facts.

"Let me give you a for instance. Suppose Mr. Grimes asks you to give him the component of profit contributed by each product. Could you do that?"

"Absolutely. I know all the components of the costs that contribute to the manufacture of every product."

"Aha, then when you allocate the costs of every worker in the factory, you assign their costs to the product they are working on? Is that right?"

"Well, not exactly. We divide the total hours of labor into the standard hours established by the MRP folks for that product and use the average labor of the factory. And . . ." Chris paused for a moment, "you got me. I see what you are saying. I am not tracking the real numbers. I am tracking the standards from the MRP system and not the real numbers. So, Mr. Grimes really doesn't know what's going on from the numbers that I give him."

"Chris, again, I am not trying to blame you. I am merely trying to get you and everyone in the company to rethink what you are doing. You need to work with the people on the shop floor to get accurate run-time figures. You need real numbers, not theoretical ones."

At that moment Mac looked up and said, "The hardest thing that happens when we work with different companies is that we have to break down barriers that various supervisers and managers have put up over the years. Chris has had a barrier around his shop. In order for him to function in the new environment, those barriers have to come down and his department has to be more approachable.

"John, your department has to provide a service to the people on the shop floor so they can use the information that you provide. Again, your barriers have to come down. We have to remove the mantle of materials czar from storeroom manager and put control where it should be."

John, who had cooled down, said, "Mac I owe an apology to you and Dr. Elbie. My computer salesman took me over to see Peter Schmit at Prescott's. I couldn't believe it. He was having fun. He was working with less pressure and everyone was in good spirits. And today, Prescott's just gave everybody their first bonus from the profit pool. They will be getting bonuses quarterly. They also are starting a profit sharing program for everyone's retirement.

"He really doesn't manage the MRP system or the MIS department. He is sort of an information guru for all the teams. He helps the different teams with measurement, the numbers they need to measure, and their needs to computerize them. Mr. Prescott put a sign on his door which read, Measurement Czar. I'm sorry for my misunderstanding earlier in the day. I am sorry for the stir I caused. Just be patient with me. I'll come around."

Mac went on, "Thanks, John. We appreciate that. We want you to play on our team." Mac and John each raised their right hands with the peace sign announcing the end of the momentary hostilities.

Mac went on, "I want to make a few points about the systems support. The six types of systems support I think you should know are:

6 Major Systems Support Types
(controlled by managers and supervisers)
1. Information
2. Rules and Policies
3. Rewards
4. Time
5. Physical Work Layout
6. Technology.

"Let me run through the first two quickly.

"One. Information. Information is very important. Managers and supervisers usually control the flow of information to their subordinates. Information flow through the organization is usually slow and in controlled amounts because *knowledge is power*, but a worker must know the results of the work as it is performed in order to judge his or her daily performance.

"Two. Rules and Policies. What we saw in our discussion earlier was a set of rules and policies that were established at some time to solve a particular problem. When John set up the MRP system, he set up some firm rules to help him get it installed and running as best he could. He got it going but *the rules and policies were getting in the way of getting the work out*. So the rules and policies have to be examined. And maybe even changed.

"In Chris's case, the rules and policies and measures were not able to give the results that would help the company executives make better decisions. Chris and the company have to rethink the rules and policies of his department to insure that the change occurs.

"To summarize, three things need to happen to make change occur. John, what are they?"

John snapped to. "Ability, willingness and systems support, sir!"

Mac responded, "Right on. Now let's quickly go through the other issues.

"Three. Rewards. All employees respond positively to rewards, but the key here is that the reward must encourage the behavior we want. If we want people to cooperate in teams, then reward them for team behavior. For example, the PRB is going to give bigger incentives for ideas coming from a team. The reward must encourage this behavior. I always like to talk to owners and CEOs who talk about teamwork, but reward their executives for individual performance. Does that create teamwork?"

Everyone shook their head as if to concede the point to Mac. "So whatever change we want to create, we drive it with the reward system. Oh yes, one other thing. Remember that all rewards aren't monetary.

"Four. Time. Excuse me for rushing these points. I'm trying to get the basic messages across and then I am going to give you an assignment. The main reason time and its control is a systems support issue is that managers must give their employees time to get the work done. Workers need to communicate effectively to work in a team. If a manager sees workers talking and tells the superviser to tell them not to talk, then the workers are getting mixed messages. You want them to work but you are not giving them *the time* to do it. Time is required to do any job well. And we are encouraging workers to improve the operation. To encourage both work and continuous improvement requires time. The system must allow time for both. If we want to change to a new culture, we must allow time for the ideas to be absorbed. When people begin asking about a job procedure, that is time that is part of the job.

"I will talk about the other two items, *Physical Work Layout* and *Technology* in the next regular VAP class. In the meantime, I want you to think about all the areas you control that will make the changes we want to happen. Is that a deal?" Everyone nodded and the group dispersed.

Over the weekend the whole family was interested in Daddy's project. Buddy wanted to look at the drawings. Sandy was excited about her idea and that it was being implemented. We actually were going to move the machine. Her idea wasn't dumb.

18

Monday rolled around quickly. Dr. Elbie was going to get us going on the discussion of lead time. Everybody was starting to pull together. We had met over the weekend for our presentation to Mr. Grimes the next Monday. We had many of the details of our cell layout pretty well defined. Tony and Gus had some other commitment over the weekend and weren't able to join us, but Phil met with us and helped quite a bit. We had figured out how we would install the ball lock system and had several fixtures already designed.

Phil said that the issues of lead time and further explanations of kanban would help us, so all of us were interested in Monday's class. As I walked through the shop that morning I noticed that something was different. It suddenly hit me that something had been moved. My table at my work area had been moved.

As I entered the meeting room, Gus and Tony were smiling. Class was just starting and they were ready for Dr. Elbie, who came in one minute late and wrote twenty-four late minutes on the board as there were twenty-four people in the room. I think we were going to win the bet with him without any problem.

As he got to the front of the class he looked at Tony and said, "Are you ready for your announcement?"

"Yes, we are." Tony stood up and said, "Over the weekend, Gus, Frank, Jim, Phil, a representative from our machinery dealer and I came in and installed the ball lock plates and system on all the milling machines in our shop. We installed the system on seventeen machines in all. We wanted to surprise everybody. It was a lot of work to keep our plan a secret. We are ready. Gentlemen, start your engines!" I hadn't seen anyone this excited in a long time. Tony and the tool and die people had succeeded in surprising us.

"We are ready to run the top fifteen jobs that we do out there. Now! We really wanted to surprise him," and Tony and Gus pointed to me. "You were our inspiration. We called this project Operation Charlie in honor of your friend. It was a success, we think, and we want you to start the first job. We'll time you and start posting the setup results as they come in on Calvin's board."

I knew the ball lock system would work. Tony and Gus had

worked hard to mill the plates, and drill ball lock holes precisely to position, and they had to do this for seventeen machines.

Tony sat down, smiling at his accomplishment. He had bags under his eyes, but he wasn't going to bed until he had seen that first setup.

Everyone's attention turned to Dr. Elbie and class resumed. I was having a hard time concentrating as I began to think of what I had to do to make the first part. Dr. Elbie asked me, "Do you remember reading *The Goal?*"*

I said, "Yes, I do."

He asked me again, "And do you remember the story about Herbie?"

Again I did, and I smiled. "I guess the answer is yes. For those of you who haven't read it, please read *The Goal*. Dr. Elbie put copies for everyone in the back of the room." Buck got up to get his copy and Dr. Elbie said, "You can pick it up after class." Buck sat down.

"The reason I want you to read the book is that there are many things of interest. The story I find most interesting tells about the hero trying to manage a group of boy scouts on a hike. How many in this room have ever tried to take a group of boys on a hike that ended in an overnight?"

Several hands went up and Dr. Elbie said, "Good, you might appreciate this story. Anyway, the hero of *The Goal* is stuck as the lone leader of a group of boy scouts. He is trying to get them to their destination and is blessed with Herbie. Every boy scout troop in America has a Herbie. He is the little fat kid who is always dragging along in the rear of any activity. You might have thirty-five world class athletes in your troop, but you somehow have to accommodate Herbie. He can't keep up with the other boys.

"So guess what? Our hero figures out a solution to the problem. As it stands, he has some boys who can cover six miles in an hour. Herbie can only walk three miles in an hour. If he lets the troop go two hours, what is our hero's problem?"

Tony knew about this. He was the leader of local troop 6. He said, "After two hours he is going to have kids spread over six miles. And believe me, that is a problem. I've usually dealt with it by telling everyone to slow down to Herbie's pace, but after a while, they get bored and start cranking it up. How does our hero solve the problem?"

---

* The Goal. A Process of Ongoing Improvement. By Eliyahu M. Goldratt and Jeff Cox.

"He puts Herbie in the front of the line. No one can pass Herbie. They can only go as fast as the slowest person. Does that relate to what goes on in the factory?"

Bonnie liked this discussion. "Yes, it does, Dr. Elbie. It is just what bottlenecks do in a factory. Herbie is just like the slowest process on the shop floor. We can't run the factory any faster than the slowest process. I still remember this from school. If we have five steps in a cycle to make an object and four steps take one minute and the fifth step takes five minutes, after a while parts stop dropping off the assembly line every five minutes. It doesn't make any difference how fast any one process is, you can't go faster than the slowest one. Just like Herbie."

Dr. Elbie clapped, "Bravo, Bonnie. Do you know what we call this process?"

She looked puzzled, but answered, Herbie Measurement?

Someone else said, "No, let's call it the Herbie Process."

Mr. Grimes bellowed out, "No, no. This is Herbie Analysis. Yes, this is Herbie Analysis."

"You're right. That's what we call it. Because it is easy for people to understand. Let's take the example Bonnie just gave. Suppose that we have five steps in a process." Dr. Elbie went to the board and wrote:

Step 1—1 Minute
Step 2—1 Minute
Step 3—5 Minutes
Step 4—1 Minute
Step 5—1 Minute.

"Now, how long will it take to make the first piece, when you start up this product line?"

"Nine minutes."

"OK. Good. Now after the first piece comes down the line, how long will it take for the second piece?"

Tony wanted to get involved in this conversation but he was tired. He said, "Nine minutes."

Dr. Elbie then asked him, "Tony, how did you arrive at that?"

"If it takes nine minutes to get the first piece through the line, it will take the same time for the second piece."

"Did you consider the queue of products that are already in line." Tony said that he didn't. Dr. Elbie went on, "Tony, walk each product through the system. When can the second piece start at the third operation?"

"Only after it is finished with the first piece." Tony paused a second, "Oh, I see it now. There is a bottleneck at the third operation and the second part will wait there for four minutes, the third part will wait . . ." and he thought a few minutes, "eight minutes. And that creates the bottleneck. I see now."

"Does everybody see this?" Dr. Elbie scanned the room and saw Buck raise his hand.

"Dr. Elbie, I see what Tony was just saying, but can't you speed the process up by moving the operation to the last step." Dr. Elbie was very patient during this whole process. You could tell that he wanted everyone to understand what was going on. He spent time showing Buck that it didn't make any difference where the bottleneck was. If it was a bottleneck, it controlled the process. So we learned that Bonnie was correct; nothing can go faster than the slowest operation.

Dr. Elbie was trying to move the discussion to a specific product. We had discussed the 255 MT on several occasions, so he picked this one again. He asked Mr. Grimes what the lead time for it was. "I think it is close to twelve weeks. We get the order and try to process it in six weeks but we are always late. Wouldn't you say that we are never on time with this product?"

Roland had missed a few classes in order to make out of town calls. He was trying to pay attention but he was distracted by something. He waited a few seconds before responding to Mr. Grimes, "Oh, we are so late with this product that we are about to lose a big customer. We missed shipping a big order on time and it caused them some credibility problems with one of their customers. If this was the first time, it wouldn't be a problem, but it happens over and over with them. We have got to do something about this."

Dr. Elbie asked what sounded like a real dumb question. "If you could solve the late shipment problem, is there any more business potential for us?"

"Oh, yes. We could double our shipment of product, if we could ship in six weeks."

"What could you do if you could ship in two weeks?"

"That's impossible, but we would have a very happy customer. A very happy Roland Diamond. I could rule the world."

Dr. Elbie smiled and said, "Then let's make Roland the emperor, and shoot for a two-week shipment goal from receipt of order."

"Now what is the actual manufacturing time for this order? How long would it take me to make one unit, from scratch, if I had all the parts I needed, if I didn't have to wait at all for any of the machines, and if my tester and paint booth were all ready for me?"

Mr. Grimes answered, "Tony and Gus, correct me if I'm wrong, but wouldn't you say about 45 minutes?"

Tony said, "No, Mr. Grimes, it would only take about 30 minutes. Many of the operations are only 10 to 15 seconds, but we have large queues at every operation. I think it would only be 30 minutes."

Dr. Elbie said, "Why don't we answer the question by actually going through the 255 MT process. Does that make sense?"

"Yes, it does. Let's do it," Tony said rather intensely. "I think the first operation on that order is operation 10, OP 10. As I read the figure, it says kit the material for the job." Tony and the class detailed the following table:

Operation	Description	Single Part Cycle Time
10	Kit material for job	1 minute
20	Move pallet to mill	3.5 minutes
	Setup job—1 hour	
	run 300 bodies—16 hours & 54 minutes	3.5 minutes
30	Move to drilling center (if more than 4 pallets at drill area move to staging area) drill and tap—lower body assembly	2.5 minutes
	drill—upper body assembly	1 minute
40	Move to boring center	7 minutes
	If more than 6 pallets, move to staging area	
50	Drill valve outlet ports—4 outlet ports	12 minutes
60	Hone Bearing sleeve	1 minute
70	Press bearing into sleeve	5 minutes
80	Move to assembly kitting area	—
	Total time upper assembly body	26 Minutes
	Total time lower assembly body	27.5 Minutes

The New Turnaround

"It looks like you are pretty close to the numbers. Where is the Herbie in this operation?"

Someone in the back yelled out, "Operation 50, drilling the valve ports."

Dr. Elbie responded, "Good. Now, how many minutes would you have between ports once you got the process going?"

Buck was into this and said, "12 minutes. Every 12 minutes a finished part should drop out of the process."

Mac jumped in, "So, Roland, if we run this plant 8 hours a day, you should get 40 255 MTs per day, or 80 on a two-shift basis. Would that make you happy?"

Roland, who was disappointed over his recent cancellation, suddenly got interested. "You mean to say that if we rethink what we are doing, we can get 40 units a day, without much effort?"

"I have my opinions on this, Roland. Does anyone have any ideas on how to give Roland his 40 units a day?"

Jim was now ready to roll. "Yes, Mac, I have an idea. Why don't we move one or two of each of the machines needed into an area that we will call the 255 MT cell. Let's line them up in a u-shape like this." And Jim went up to the board and drew the following arrangement.

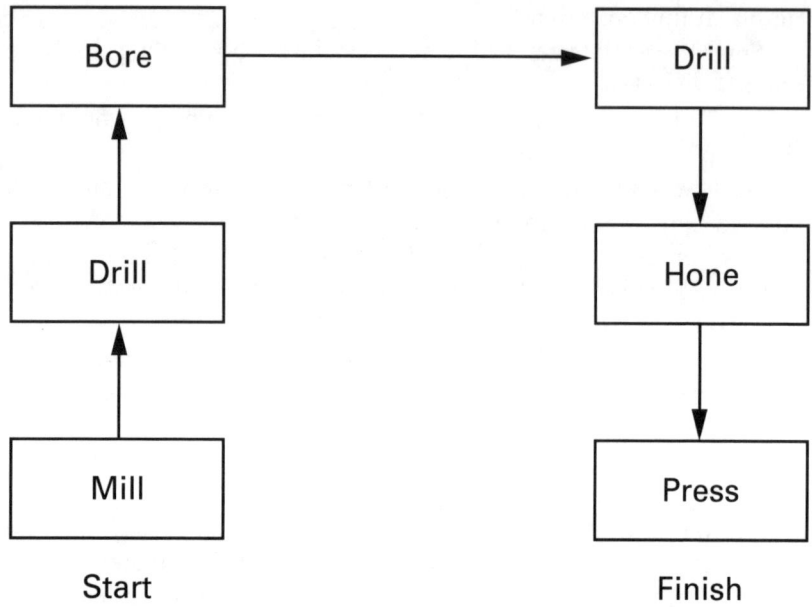

255 MT Cell Layout

Jim went on, "If we moved all of these units to this arrangement and don't change a single step in the process we will get phenomenal throughput out of the cell. Not only that, we won't need to worry about setup because we can leave the equipment setup permanently fixed to run 255 MT's."

Mr. Grimes was sitting over in the corner shaking his head. "Why didn't I think of that earlier? What about all the different variations of the 255 MT valve arrangements?"

Mac looked at the class. "This isn't my project. Do any of you have any ideas to help Mr. Grimes?"

Frank had been quiet for most of the sessions. Whenever he spoke, everyone paid attention. Frank began, "You know Mr. Grimes, I have been listening to this discussion for several weeks now and I just laugh. You wouldn't listen to me several years ago when I made this same suggestion. There isn't really anything new here. It's just that you are listening to us now."

Frank had gotten that off his chest and now he was ready to talk. "The 255 MT is easy to change over from one unit to the next. I don't think any of the fixtures or jigs would take more than five or ten minutes to change from one version of the 255 MT to another. I think we should move the equipment immediately. Since Roland is having a problem with the customer, let's make this change and get more business."

Frank turned and looked at Roland. "I think Roland should buy us all beer and pizza when we get this new arrangement installed. He should be able to afford it." Frank smiled and finished with, "Let's put this on the top of Calvin's priority list. As I see it, this change is no more than $1,000 to move the equipment. The increased revenue potential is big. So in Calvin's analysis, the cost is $1,000, the benefit would be increased sales of . . ."

Roland jumped in, "I think we would ship at least $500,000 in more units if we can deliver. So from my perspective the benefit is an increase in sales of $500,000. Lord knows what the waste elimination would be. Inventory would certainly go down, WIP would go down. Damnit, let's do it. It seems that it certainly offers a low risk and a high probability of success, and it certainly is consistent with the mission of the company. If that isn't an A-A then I don't know where it would be. Let's do it!"

Roland was speaking of the cost-benefit, mission relevance check lists. An A-A was the low cost-high benefit, high mission relevance-high probability of success project. It was clear that this was a go.

Dr. Elbie interjected, "Calvin, I think Roland is in favor of this project. I would probably give this a high priority. What do you think?"

Calvin wanted to help in any way he could and said that all the electrical wiring could be arranged to start tomorrow and the moving could be done on Saturday. So he said, "We would be ready to go next Monday. We might need to buy some additional tools but I think this is pretty simple. Roland, if this old customer is interested, we can run the cell for a week and then bring the customer in. Maybe we can move assembly over to that area and start to work on that at the same time. If we do the assembly and testing right off the end of the manufacturing line, we won't waste any time. If I remember correctly, the people in assembly made the calculation and they figured that three assembly and test people could produce one pump every ten minutes. We might as well begin to do this right now."

Mr. Grimes was surprised, "You mean to tell me that the assembly crew knows how long it should take to put together a pump. If I understand this, we can now manufacture and assemble one 255 MT every ten to twelve minutes. And we wouldn't be changing any of our processes?"

Calvin interrupted him, "You are going to have to hear that presentation from the people in assembly next week. They will knock your socks off. They are going to explain a terrific kanban technique to do assembly. You will be impressed, I am confident."

"My, my, I forgot about that," Mr. Grimes sighed. "I didn't tell all of you but Hank Thompson, the chairman of the bank that we do business with, is going to be judging the presentations with me. I told him what we were doing and he was very interested in coming over to spend a day with us. He has several clients who could use your help, Mac. It might be a better day for you than us."

Mac smiled. "Thank you, John. Jack and I would enjoy meeting him." And Mac turned to the class and said, "See you next Monday. If you have any last-minute questions about any of your presentation materials, you can reach Dr. Elbie or me at our homes during the week. Feel free to give us a call." Mac wrote their home phone numbers on the board for all of us to copy in our notebooks. We did and left the classroom.

19

We worked on our presentation during the rest of the week and over the weekend. On Monday morning everyone was excited about the presentations and there was a certain amount of competition among all the classes. We were called up first in the random draw. Mr. Grimes and Mr. Thompson were in their seats ready to go.

As we agreed, Gus and Tony would go first. They wanted to give the part of the presentation on the ball lock system and how it had been working. Tony began, "We have the first presentation of the day, and as you will find out, we are going to be the best. My good friend and associate here is going to give you the facts on the very successful implementation of the ball lock system. It serves as the basis of how we are going to make this new enhanced pump system, the most successful product introduced in the history of this company."

Tony introduced Gus, who wasn't as comfortable as Tony but got over his initial butterflies and began his presentation. "In the last week, we did forty setups on the seventeen machines that we converted to the ball lock system."

Mr. Thompson was not bashful and asked Gus to explain how a ball lock worked. Gus was great. He walked back to Mr. Thompson and in just a few minutes explained its operation clearly and succinctly to him. He continued. "For jobs that had to be converted to use the ball-lock system, no setup was over two hours. We averaged about an hour for the forty setups. For those same jobs, before the system was installed, the average setup was over five hours."

Gus and Tony sat down. They had presented their material on overhead transparencies they had made themselves. During the training, they had learned to use an Apple Macintosh computer to prepare their slides. I was up next.

I went over the new product design with Frank and Bonnie as support. We discussed that we were going to make the new product in the cell discussed in class. Over the weekend the machines had been moved into position and the cell was ready for production. We explained the waste eliminated due to manufacturing products in the cell arrangement. We felt that we could integrate the assembly operation right into the cell. The assembly crew was going to discuss the specifics of the assembly part of the operation in their presentation. We included an overview of what the completed cell would look like.

We calculated that the machine capacity would allow us to make one of the new pumps every six minutes. Roland got up and went over the implications of that capability. He felt that this would improve his potential to capture some big clients. If we could manufacture the product at the rate we were projecting, we would easily be in a dominant market position.

One of the problems we anticipated was slack time in the demand for the new product. Did we make the product for finished inventory or wait for orders? We figured we would be creating significant inventory costs for the company if we made products to fill an uncertain forecast. Roland said that if we had the capacity we were projecting, the sales department could handle the logistics of getting products to customers.

As we ended our presentation, Mr. Thompson clapped enthusiastically. I gathered from some of his comments that he was going to be able to relax a little concerning the loan obligations of Quality Pump. I could see why Mr. Grimes had him attend. After the other two teams made their presentations, Mr. Thompson asked to address the class.

"Ladies and Gentlemen, I am impressed. You all did such a fine job that it will be difficult to decide a winner, but we will come to some conclusions. I can see how this process can turn around an organization quickly.

"We have a few minutes, let's talk about one of my problems. I would be interested in your input." Everyone looked around the room. We were now getting into the banking business! That was interesting. Dr. Elbie indicated that this process worked at banks and insurance companies. Well, this might be fun.

"Here is the problem. It takes me three weeks to process loans at the bank. What do I do?"

Buck was in the back; he paced whenever he got excited about something. He said, "Mr. Thompson, you can do exactly what we did. You identify the wastes, you cost them out, you figure who adds value, and you look at different solutions. First you have to find where the waste is!"

Mr. Thompson responded, "OK, I can follow that. There is waste in waiting for documents, there is waste in waiting for signatures, there is waste in waiting for the loan applicant to get the loan papers to us."

We didn't have much time but we figured out that they wasted a

The New Turnaround

lot of time in getting the loan documents all prepared. They waited until all the documents were in a little binder before starting to process the loan. As we progressed in our few minutes, we agreed that value was only contributed by those people who signed the documents. Mr. Thompson was having fun. By the end of the day he might even get a problem solved. He had written all the information on the flip chart and was going to expand it. We made our presentations and had helped a bank executive rethink his business.

Class ended and Mr. Grimes and Mr. Thompson were going to have a busy day. They had to listen to three presentations per class.

The class with the assemblers had figured out a way to insure that they would never run out of the nuts and bolts and little stuff that keeps them from getting orders out the door. They worked with John Alphonse to use the MRP system to set up primary storage locations for the parts on the shop floor. The secondary locations were going to be the central stores.

As I understood their plan, they were going to use kanban boxes to signal a need to fill an empty container. When they needed to fill the box, the assemblers would put it on top of the rack. A runner was going to take it over to stores and fill it. John Alphonse figured out that the kanban box would have a card on it. The card would have all the information on the parts in the box. When the box was empty the card would be fed into the MRP system to tell it that the primary location had consumed one bin of goodies. That might be twenty-five items or a hundred units or a thousand units depending upon the part.

Nuts and bolts were going to be weighed. They would use the scale in stores to weigh out the right amount of bolts when the box was empty. That would be fed into the system and the stores inventory would be adjusted. John was really proud of what he was able to contribute. From what we had heard John and the people from assembly had given a great presentation. John was able to make the MRP system serve our needs in the factory. We no longer were serving him. We were now the *point of control.*

At the end of the day Mr. Grimes and Mr. Thompson caucased in the conference room. Pizza was warming in the truck that was parked outside. We waited and Mr. Grimes and Mr. Thompson came down the aisle to the back dock. Buck had prepared a podium for their presentation.

Everyone assembled in front of the podium and Mr. Grimes began, "I would like to thank all of you for putting in such a fine effort to get your materials ready for these presentations. There were no bad presentations, in fact, they were all quite good. Hank Thompson will make the announcement. Hank." And Mr. Grimes greeted him with a handshake as he approached the podium.

Mr. Thompson began, "I must admit that I have had to spend some days doing a lot of boring things. Today was not one of them. This was probably the most exciting time I have had in business for a long time. You were all marvelous. You have such great enthusiasm for your work and your confidence of your future success is most encouraging.

"As many of you know, I have the largest investment in Quality Pump of any of Mr. Grimes's bankers. I have a vested interest in seeing you succeed. My comfort level is very high right now. If you implement the projects you have proposed, Mr. Grimes and my stockholders will be very happy.

"By the way, I really enjoyed working with you in solving my problem. I guess that I will have Jack Elbie educate my people just as he did you. My eyes were opened today. Thanks again for your help.

"Now for the winner or winners." Everyone looked around. There was only supposed to be one winner. "Mr. Grimes and I couldn't decide on one project, so we decided on two." Mr. Thompson didn't waste any time. "We liked the new product project of Class 1 and the assembly project of Class 5. We liked both of them because if you implement them both you will be able to apply the concept of cells to other products. I can see the real possibilities in inventory reduction, lead-time reduction, quality improvement and Roland Diamond's coronation." Some of us laughed. Our class was the only group that really understood. Mr. Thompson caught on and explained, "I understand that this design will make Roland a lot of money on commissions. Good. That is what this whole concept is about: making more money for everybody."

Everybody clapped, but Mr. Thompson wasn't finished. "Doesn't anyone want to know about my project?" Everyone was more interested in pizza, but they understood that he had taken a day to spend with us and we could afford to give him a few more minutes. "Let me say that we came up with a good solution. As I understand it, you are recommending that each loan document for each person requesting a loan of over five hundred thousand dollars get a separate treatment by the staff.

"The income tax forms will go through one path, the loan applica-

The New Turnaround

tion will go through another. Each separate loan document's path will have value-adding signatures. And there will also be people who need to know about some information. They will only get copies of the documents. And finally, when the last document is still not in from the client, we will be on our toes waiting. As soon as it hits the bank, we will process that *last* document within twenty-four hours. That, my friends, is a marvelous solution."

Someone in the back said, "Mr. Thompson, make sure the idea comes from the people, not you. That way it will be their idea."

Mr. Thompson laughed and stepped back from the podium. He gained his composure and said, "You know, I have to admit that before today, I probably wouldn't have. Now, I will. Thank you very much again. I loved it. Good luck. I'll stop by in a couple of weeks to see how you are doing."

Everyone clapped again and immediately turned to the pizza, which had been brought into the room.

Mac and Dr. Elbie were over talking to Mr. Thompson when Phil came up. Phil shook hands with Mr. Thompson and they all were apparently getting ready to take on a job with Mr. Thompson's bank.

Calvin and I were standing over by the PRB results board when I looked up at the board. Someone had put a sign up on the bulletin board in big letters: Darth Vader Lives. He is human!!

It had been done on a Mac and I knew immediately who had done it. I smiled at Calvin. He had no clue.

Conclusion

Six months later—I pulled my pickup into the parking lot and took my usual place. As I started to get out, a green, battered Volvo station wagon pulled up beside me. It was Dr. Elbie. He smiled through the window, gave a brief wave and opened the door. He reached back into the car and grabbed his briefcase. He stood up and asked if he could walk with me.

We headed to the back entrance when Buck squealed his tires as he pulled into the lot and brought the car to an abrupt halt in his place by the dock. He jumped out and yelled at Dr. Elbie, "Hey, Elbie, we did it!"

Dr. Elbie was taken aback and asked, "Did what, Buck?"

We got our schedule down for the last three months and haven't been late once. You owe us pizza. Only this time we want Gino's. We're going uptown on you this time."

Apparently, Dr. Elbie had lost a bet to Buck and the shipping crew that they couldn't post a weekly schedule and stick to it every day for three months. Dr. Elbie lost but he didn't seem to mind the expense. Buck and his crew had really become a strong support team in the organization.

As Dr. Elbie and I entered the back door, various guys were coming over to ask Dr. Elbie to visit them later in the morning to see some new improvement in their operation. It was amazing! Just six months ago, I thought that Quality Pump was dead. The change was dramatic and you could see that Dr. Elbie was proud of what he and Mac had done. It was a real transformation.

We talked for a minute and I headed over to the team leaders to see if everything was OK for the day. Five teams had been formed around the different product lines and the whole organization was designed to support these teams. It was really amazing!

The logic was simple. Define the value-adding work and design the organization around appropriate work teams to optimize the profits and quality. It really was simple. The engineers were no longer obstacles. They worked right along with all of us to keep track of the new products as they moved through the system. The improvements in all aspects of the work were going on daily. If we needed to make any

The New Turnaround

new acquisitions of equipment, we studied the market for new equipment, decided the contribution to profit from the acquisition (return on investment/payback) and argued our case to the executive staff (through the PRB) if the acquisition was not in our planned budget.

Everyone was enjoying the new environment. However, a couple of the guys really didn't like the team business. It turns out that teams expose your weaknesses quickly. Several of the guys couldn't deliver the quality that was needed by one of the teams and ended up being transferred to another team. Mac had mentioned once that teams were far more severe on non-performers than any other form of management. The team polices itself. Everyone has a job to do and is expected to deliver. If a member of the team needs help, the other members of the team will lobby for support. But if the person is unable or unwilling to hold up his or her end of the defined work, the other members can be ruthless. Tardiness is not tolerated, absenteeism is not tolerated, poor quality is not tolerated. Once the team agrees on its standards, everyone must contribute. There are no excuses. On the other hand, there is no blame. If you need help, ask. It works very well.

Dr. Elbie excused himself and headed up to see Mr. Grimes. As I watched him go to the front office, a number of workers interrupted him to see various improvements. The programmer showed him the new computer and how he could see where each job was in the shop. The assembly group showed him the new table arrangement. And so it went as he walked up to the front.

He entered the front office and began to hear various clerks pointing out wastes that had been eliminated since his last visit two weeks earlier. As he entered Mr. Grimes' office, Roland Diamond was sitting in one of the chairs. He got up to shake Dr. Elbie's hand and Mr. Grimes reached across the desk to do the same. They smiled at each other for a second and Roland said, "Dr. Elbie, you know that we have gotten the backlog down and can now deliver 90% of the products in the catalog on two days notice. We have 3 months advance orders and we are shipping 100% of orders on schedule."

He was almost out of breath as he gloated, "and you know, Dr. Elbie, Quality Pump is now a certified supplier to three air conditioning companies with the new product. We have won the last four competitive bids and we always win after we bring the client to visit the plant. Last week, we had our salesman in Texas bring the client in with a special order and we let him follow the product from the receipt of the order to the completion in assembly. It was a special order and it was handled like clockwork. He was impressed, to say the least. We got a $1.2 million order as a result."

You could tell that Roland was excited, "Dr. Elbie, I have to go. But thanks, again. If you need any references put me on the top of the list, of course, after Mr. Grimes." Roland shook Dr. Elbie's hand and headed out the door. Dr. Elbie turned to Mr. Grimes and they both sat down.

Mr. Grimes reached into his drawer and pulled out a folder. He placed it on the desk in front of Dr. Elbie. He nodded for Dr. Elbie to pick it up. As he did so the phone rang and Mr. Grimes answered it after the second ring. He had a call from a new prospect and had to take it. As he began talking, Dr. Elbie picked up the folder and began to read. It was good news. The year-end financials were complete. Last year the company had shown a loss of 9% on sales of $18 million. In the last seven months the sales had increased and the net revenue for the year was $23.5 million with a profit of 15%. The most exciting part of the news was that the pre-tax profit for the last quarter was 26% of sales and the last month showed a pre-tax profit of 31%. Inventory was down to $1.4 million and it was clear that the $1 million level was within reach. There was not much information on profitability because they were trying to get a good handle on the efficiency numbers and the value of the waste of human potential. After about a year, these numbers on profitability might start to make more sense.

Mr. Grimes hung up the phone and looked at Dr. Elbie, "Pretty good, huh?"

Dr. Elbie looked up, "Not bad, not bad. Where are you going from here?"

Mr. Grimes said, "You know better than me. Where do I go from here? Calvin seems to be getting things under control. Roland is excited for the first time in a long, long time. Everyone is moving forward with their ideas. I can't think of much more that we can do."

Dr. Elbie sat up, and he looked at Mr. Grimes with an almost puzzled look. He then said, "So you've created Kansas City and you've gone about as fer as you can go."

"Well, I didn't mean that we can't improve. I mean that our system of continuous improvement seems to be working. I know we need to keep it going and we need to set new goals for ourselves. But I know that we are all focused and are going in the same direction. Jack, I've been thinking about this since we started the project.

The New Turnaround

"It's clear to me that we have been able to get the whole organization from the bottom up to support the suggestions for improvement. Most of those ideas were from our own employees, who implemented suggestions for improvement that they developed. The ideas were their own and they made them work. That much is clear. But I guess I am amazed by how quickly and efficiently the whole process worked. Why is that?"

Dr. Elbie smiled and responded, "You know the answer and I'm surprised that you would ask me. We've talked about it before."

Mr. Grimes acknowledged the previous discussion and went on, "I know that you said it but I have a hard time believing that it is so easy. I guess you are looking for the basis of our discussion of over six months ago. I remember you saying that this process works for a number of reasons, but one was that this process attended to the system, the business system, as a whole. You didn't just analyze manufacturing or sales or engineering, you treated them as a system and dealt with that. But is it that simple?"

Dr. Elbie answered, "In a way it is. Most consulting approaches isolate one or the other of the departments, and solutions that arise out of those programs are at best patches. By attending to the whole system, everyone is drawn into the process at the same time and singular issues are seen as what they really are, problems with the whole system.

Most efforts to change organization performance, whether they are directed from inside the organization or from without, through some sort of program, or through consulting help, are rarely based on a system view. Instead, the emphasis is on improving production, reducing inventory, increasing quality, etc., without a plan to treat all the interacting aspects of the organization that affect the target issue, group, or function. We believe this won't be truly effective, because no group or function operates in a vacuum, and no problem affects only a portion of the organization.

"Mac thinks of this as a sports team analogy. It wouldn't make sense to say that you are going to improve the passing game on a football team by working only with the blocking backs. You would, of course, work with the whole team to change the way all parts of the team function in passing situations. That's what we do—work with the whole organization. And that's why we mixed the classes the way we did.

"Thus, we always begin our work with clients by helping *everyone* in the organization understand exactly how the system currently works. That could mean, for example, that in a manufacturing company we would begin by exploring with everyone present what happens, step by step, from the moment a customer calls about a prospective order, to the moment that a check arrives to pay for the completed products. That is what we did with the Process Map. We have yet to find a single company in which *anyone,* including managers, understood all the steps that took place. Until the existing system is understood, changing it is a real struggle. And again, that's what we found here."

Mr. Grimes took over, "I am amazed at this conversation. First of all, I am enjoying it, but six months ago, I would have cut you off so that I could get back to work.

"I have to admit that it is really an odd thing that you do. I never would have thought of approaching business improvement by focusing on the work and not on the people. My wife was telling me the other day that she had seen a show on television that discussed the same issue but from the perspective of a psychiatrist who was treating disturbed people. His observation was that it was easier to treat the surroundings of the disturbed individual, including the patients support group at home, than it was the individual. As she told me this, I could see the similarity to what happened at Quality Pumps. You dealt with the work environment and the desired employee behavior followed. That may be stretching, but I think it helped me understand what happened here."

Dr. Elbie responded, "What you are saying is one of the most interesting of the observations of VAP. The effort to improve the organization's performance must begin with clarity as to the right work to do. Everything else flows from that revelation. First, determine the way the system works now, then pinpoint the wastes (the activities that add no value) and then mount a campaign to eliminate *all* waste in the system. As the value-adding process is clarified, the work itself then dictates the roles, tasks, jobs, relationships, and yes, even behavior, that must support the right work.

Mr. Grimes jumped in, "I see it now. If the organization is to use teams, self-managing work groups, open communication, or flat management structures, such use will flow from an understanding of what adds value and what does not. As I recall you saying, *The work leads, and the people follow.*"